The Crafty Poet II

Also by Diane Lockward

The Uneaten Carrots of Atonement
Temptation by Water
What Feeds Us
Eve's Red Dress

Greatest Hits: 1997-2010 (chapbook)
Against Perfection (chapbook)

The Crafty Poet: A Portable Workshop

The Crafty Poet II
A Portable Workshop

edited by

Diane Lockward

Terrapin Books

Published by Terrapin Books
4 Midvale Avenue
West Caldwell, NJ 07006

terrapinbks@gmail.com

www.terrapinbooks.com

ISBN: 978-0-9969871-7-2
LCCN: 2016905339

First edition

The editor thanks the poets who contributed their work to this book. She also thanks the publishers who generously made the poems available to her. Finally, she thanks the loyal subscribers to her monthly Poetry Newsletter who motivated her to write this sequel to the original *The Crafty Poet: A Portable Workshop*.

Contents

III. Choosing the Right Words

VI. Adding Complication

IX. Expanding the Material

Introduction

After the publication of the original *The Crafty Poet: A Portable Workshop*, I thought that would be my one and only craft book. However, I continued sending out my monthly Poetry Newsletter, which had provided the material for the first book, and I continued saving the new material. As my desktop folder began to bulge with additional poems, prompts, and craft tips, I realized that a companion volume was certainly a possibility.

The success of the first volume encouraged me to proceed. The book had worked its way into college and university classrooms across the US, as well as in Canada, the UK, and even the Virgin Islands. It had also found a place as a working text in numerous workshops. Individuals working alone at home wrote and told me they'd found the book useful for improving their knowledge of craft and stimulating new poems; with the book in hand, they were able to work effectively even in isolation.

Eventually, I printed out the material that had accumulated since the publication of the first volume. I went through that massive pile and began to organize it into sections by concept. As I did so, I realized that the new book, *The Crafty Poet II*, was a natural extension of the material in the original book and that it would pick up where the first book left off. Readers who have the original book will soon see that *The Crafty Poet II* is a logical companion and follow-up, but, like the original, can also stand on its own.

Like the original, *The Crafty Poet II* is organized into ten sections. We again end with "Revision," but this time we also begin with it in "Revising Your Process." That section is followed by one on "Entryways into Poems" which considers how a poet might get going with a poem and how a poet might pull in a reader with humor and enticing titles. There is further but more in-depth discussion of the importance of choosing the right words; using syntax, line breaks, and spacing to advantage; and enhancing the music of poems.

There is now a meaty section on how to add complication to your poems, another on how to divert or transform your poems from their original intention, and another on special forms of poems. In "Expanding the Material" three poets consider how to write poetic sequences using paintings, photographs, and history. The final section, "Revision," moves beyond the usual advice to "get rid of adjectives" as one poet offers ways to revise via sound, another offers a series of expansion strategies, and, finally, poet Dick Allen issues a warning against excessive revision.

All ten sections in this book include three craft tips, each provided by an experienced, accomplished poet. Each of these thirty craft tips is followed by a Model Poem and a Prompt based on the poem. Each model poem is used as a mentor, again expressing the underlying philosophy of the first book that the best teacher of poetry is a good poem. You will find that the model poems receive more analysis than in the first book and that the prompts are a bit more challenging. Each prompt is followed by two Sample Poems contributed by subscribers to my newsletter. These sample poems, most published here for the first time, suggest the possibilities for the prompts and should provide for good discussion about what works and what doesn't. The last sample poems in each section are followed by "The Poet on the Poem" which includes a Q&A about the craft elements in one of the featured poet's poems. These Q&As generally match up with their section concept, but there is inevitably a good deal of overlap. Each section concludes with a Bonus Prompt, each of which provides a stimulus on those days when you just can't get your engine started; each bonus prompt also provides practice of a poetry skill.

I am grateful to the poets who contributed their work to *The Crafty Poet II*. A diverse group, they are spread out across the US and represent a wide range of contemporary voices and styles. A total of sixty-five poets contributed the craft tips, model poems, and Q&A poems. Of these poets, sixteen are current or former state poets laureate. An additional forty-seven poets contributed the sample poems. This group includes two former state poets laureate. Collectively, the poets have amassed an impressive number of awards, including NEA and Guggenheim fellowships, Pushcart Prizes, and Pulitzers.

The Crafty Poet II, like the original book, acts on the belief that craft can be taught and learned, both inside and outside of the classroom. Wherever you are and whether you are working in a group or by yourself, I hope that you will find this book informative and challenging. I hope that it will spark new poems from your pen.

So what are you waiting for? Get your pen ready and begin.

Diane Lockward

I. Revising Your Process

Amateurs sit and wait for inspiration;
the rest of us just get up and go to work.

—Stephen King

Craft Tip #1: One Brick at a Time

—David Kirby

The best thing a poet can do is keep a *bits journal*. A bits journal is just that; it's a collection of random images, dreams, childhood memories, snatches of overheard conversations, quotations from books you've read or lectures you've heard, bathroom graffiti, mistranslations, thoughts that come out of left field, notes to yourself, and so on.

You can't write poems every day, but you can write in your bits journal every day. This really takes the pressure off as you don't have to write memorably in your bits journal—you just have to write.

For that reason, you should never censor yourself. If you're trying to write a poem, you might say, *Oh, that's not appropriate* or *No one could ever make a decent poem of that*. But when you're writing bits, you throw in everything. Will a particular bit start moving toward poemhood? If so, fine. And if not, that's fine, too. A bit might not be useful to you for a couple of years. Or it might never be useful, but that's okay as well. It's not as though you wasted any time on it. It's not a poem, after all—it's a bit.

If you don't keep a bits journal, start today, and if you do, go back and have a look and see what you can use and what you might add. How you handle your bits journal is up to you, but I know I get antsy if my bits journal grows beyond twenty pages or so.

When that happens, it's harvest time: I'll look for bits that speak to each other, maybe three or four that might coalesce into a poem. It's said that Walt Whitman had a box of a certain size that he filled with scraps of paper on which he'd written something, and when the box filled, he'd pull out the scraps and look to see which ones would become a sequence and which he might use in another poem or return to the box.

If this method was good enough for Whitman, it's good enough for us, right? The only difference is that, instead of a box, you'll be using the bits file on your computer. I used to suggest that poets keep old-fashioned paper bits journals, but now I suggest that they make them Word documents. That way, when one bit wants to cozy up to another, you just cut and paste.

Occasionally, someone will say they have writer's block, but that's a fictitious disease. The phrase suggests that there's an immense warehouse of materials you can't get into, but the fact is that people who say they have writer's block have an empty warehouse. The bits journal is your warehouse, and it's easy to fill. If you add three or four bits a week, in a couple of months your journal will be five or six pages long, which is more than enough material to make several poems.

Poem and Prompt

Numbers

I like the generosity of numbers.
The way, for example,
they are willing to count
anything or anyone:
two pickles, one door to the room,
eight dancers dressed as swans.

I like the domesticity of addition—
add two cups of milk and stir—
the sense of plenty: six plums
on the ground, three more
falling from the tree.

And multiplication's school
of fish times fish,
whose silver bodies breed
beneath the shadow
of a boat.

Even subtraction is never loss,
just addition somewhere else:
five sparrows take away two,
the two in someone else's
garden now.

There's an amplitude to long division,
as it opens Chinese take-out
box by paper box,
inside every folded cookie
a new fortune.

And I never fail to be surprised
by the gift of an odd remainder,
footloose at the end:

forty-seven divided by eleven equals four,
with three remaining.

Three boys beyond their mothers' call,
two Italians off to the sea,
one sock that isn't anywhere you look.

—Mary Cornish

Who says poetry and math don't go together? Mary Cornish creates a lovely poem based on numbers, a topic she announces in her title and again in the single sentence of the first line. She uses first person which seems appropriate for expressing her fondness for numbers.

Not surprisingly, the poem has a logical organizational plan. The concept of numbers is broken down into the four operations that every child learns in elementary school. Cornish goes through each of these operations one by one.

Notice what's going on with sentences. The first stanza begins with a simple declarative sentence. The rest of the stanza is one additional sentence. Each stanza thereafter is one sentence only. Each sentence contains a list of examples and images. Three of these lists are introduced by a colon, generally considered a non-poetic punctuation mark.

For your own poem you are going to use the concept of numbers. As Cornish has already used the four operations to organize her poem, avoid doing that in your poem. Perhaps you might zero in on just one of the operations. Or you might choose a particular number, e.g., three. Then work solely with that number. Think of all the things that come in your number: three stooges, three musketeers, three blind mice. What could you do with 101 dalmatians? or six geese a-laying? Perhaps you might use multiples of a number: 3, 6, 9, 12, 15.

Use first person, but try not to say *I* more than three times. Begin your draft with a simple declarative sentence. Use examples and images—lots of them. Use a few colons.

As you revise, try for the one sentence per stanza plan.

Sample Poems

Six

The number of feet to dig for a coffin.
The highest roll of the dice.
The symbol of Venus, goddess of love.
The atomic number of carbon.
As a prefix, either *hex* or *sex*.
A group of French composers in the 1920s.

The crystal structure of ice.
Equal to the letters M, N and O.
A senator's term of office.
A bright red stop sign.
The most efficient shape for circuits.
The waxy architecture of the honeycomb.

The smallest positive integer
that is neither a square number
or a prime number. The age
I started the first grade. The number
of points on a Star of David. The number
of days it took to create the world.

—Kim Roberts

Dear Absolute Certainty,

Here's a domain just for you: *math.com*,
prisms and pyramids, area of a polygon,

the power of *x*. Like Prince said, *I guess
I shoulda known*, only I didn't, or not enough

about classifying angles, congruent figures,
the formula for volume. Thank you, *2piR,*

2a + 2b, for certain beyond unquestionable,
for the stupefying quiz at unit's end.

You call it a root; I'll call it a clothesline.
Together we'll get the dishes done,

and no one will go home empty-place-
holdered. My eclipse, my unknown,

I'm honoring you with a pair of forever
lines, with a co-sin I've just replaced

with a conundrum. Dear Pythagoras/
nebulous, this triangle's got three legs—

one's the curlicue of a question mark,
the others dangle like the legs of a wasp.

I should be backing slowly away,
but I guess I must be dumb like a frog pond

dusted with pollen. Wanting to thank you,
but instead I'm falling backwards

into a cloud like a giant mutt—though wait,
now it's a pair of pterosaurs, a skull.

> —Martha Silano
> published in *Redheaded Stepchild*

Craft Tip #2: The Time Is Always Right: Poetry As Escape Hatch

—Mary Biddinger

Scene A: The writer drifts into her studio at the opportune moment (whatever time of day that might be, based on personal preference) and is greeted by gently billowing curtains that reveal (insert an inspiring landscape here—it could be a mountainside, or cityscape, or field blanketed in fog). Her favorite caffeinated beverage has cooled to the ideal temperature, and she settles down into a desk chair with admirable lumbar support, ready to pen some verses. Her clothes are both comfortable and flattering. The room is (deliciously silent / blessed by the clang of distant wind chimes / primed with the poignant lyrics of Joni Mitchell). Before beginning, the writer pages through her journal and allows the perfect conditions to welcome the muse into the room.

Scene B: The writer impatiently googles on her phone: *How to remove sweet potato stain from blouse*, then adds, *on the go*. The youngest child has forgotten his lunch in the back seat, so it's another trip to school before resizing the cells of an Excel spreadsheet in advance of the morning's three-hour meeting. The writer realizes there's a sticky note clinging to her pants. It reads: *Observable Outcomes*. She reaches into her bag for a carton of yogurt, and finds instead a small tub of margarine. At least she won't have to eat her yogurt using the lid as a spoon today. A car drives by blasting a Steely Dan song that takes her back to a wild camping trip in 1988. She minimizes the spreadsheet, flips to the notes app on her phone, and starts drafting a poem.

*

Writing poetry is like a hot affair. On the screen, or in a novel, there's always a perfect time and a convenient place with silk sheets waiting. The reality of writing, however, is much like the reality of love. It is completely possible to accommodate your inspired body to a vinyl couch in the Toyota dealership lobby (hungry for the lunch you missed, ignoring urgent text queries from colleagues) and to write the poem that has been simmering inside of you. If poetry is a product of compression and condensation, then perhaps we should begin welcoming all forces to the process, including mundane and ordinarily negative pressures such as non-poetry deadlines, routine screenings, spreadsheets, and unpleasant yet inevitable phone calls.

Have you ever driven past a wind farm? Consider external energies to be the wind and your writerly self to be the turbine. This isn't a stretch; wind turbines are robust and graceful, and I recommend adding them to your daily meditation. While waiting in line at the pharmacy, gaze at the bottles behind the counter and imagine yourself as that turbine, harnessing the elements and translating them into usable poetry energy. As perfect as it might be to have designated writing time with all the traditionally necessary accessories, poetry is as much about stored energy as it is about accessing language at the right time.

Please keep this final recommendation a secret from those who might assess your performance or seek to quantify the measures of your productivity: Poetry can be an escape hatch. It takes practice and the aforementioned stockpiled energy, but it is possible to find inspiration, escape, and perhaps even writing time, on the sly. Whoever invented multiple windows on a computer was likely a poet with a day job, someone who needed to take a fifteen-minute poem break to get away from the doldrums of data entry. Beyond the computer, there's the seldom celebrated scrap of paper, which can hold two or more stanzas of freshly scribbled poetry or a knockout title for a future poem, in addition to a grocery list or phone number.

The world offers us so many distractions and reasons not to write. We need to fight back. As you stand shoulder to shoulder in solidarity with other poets on our figurative wind farm, please know that even the most perfect writing times and spaces can be subject to interruptions or diminished inspiration. When feeling pushed away from poetry, locate your nearest emergency exit and break free.

Poem and Prompt

Dear Yellow Speed Bump

One summer night a friend, on a dare,
played your game with other friends,
lying down across the narrow mountain road
and telling their best secrets. First kiss,

first time at sex. The game went smoothly,
I'm told, and so did the wine, but the secrets
were slow in coming, until one coaxed
the next, fact losing speed to fiction.

If only each day had its defining moment:
a subtle rise to catch a body off-guard
and lift it in serenity or jar it to attention
as we all wheel down the crowded road

trying to get somewhere, anywhere, fast,
when what we really want to do
is lay our burdens down on the loneliest
path and tell our only story to the stars.

—Susan Laughter Meyers

Here we have an epistolary poem, i.e., one that has the semblance
of a letter. The poet employs apostrophe as her speaker addresses
something that is non-human.

I admire the poem's symmetry. Its four quatrains and fairly even
line lengths make the poem visually attractive and give us a sense
of order. As we read the poem, we realize that this sense of order
is at odds with the poem's content. What could be riskier than
lying down on a dark and narrow mountain road?

Notice the turn that occurs midway through the poem. The *If only* that begins stanza 3 makes it possible for the poem to move to its stunning conclusion as the speed bump is transformed into the *subtle rise* of each day's *defining moment*. The turn phrase makes it possible for Meyers to move us into metaphor.

Notice also the poem's diction, e.g., *slow in coming, fact losing speed to fiction,* and *as we all wheel down the crowded road.* Meyers brings in the language of the road and driving.

Your job is to write an epistolary poem. Choose something out of the ordinary and non-human to address, e.g., a mirror, book, coat, doorknob, or rock.

Begin with "Dear _____." This salutation can be your title or your first line. Once you get the salutation down, just keep writing. Continue to use apostrophe by speaking directly to your subject.

After you have been writing for about 10-15 minutes, insert a turn word or phrase such as *but, or, if only, though,* or *and yet.* Pick up with that and keep going for another 10-15 minutes.

In revision, try a symmetrical format. Have the same number of lines per stanza as you have stanzas. For example, you might have five 5-line stanzas, four 4-line stanzas, or three 3-line stanzas.

Sample Poems

Dear Purple Bearded Iris

Welcome again, you frilly froth
of blossom next to the pond's
black water. On time, you show up
every year. Same place, no promise

needed. Well rooted, you push up
through the cold, dry soil, right after
the loud daffodils have wilted.
You don't tell me, *I'm better, watch out!*

like some who've come this way to list
my faults and flops. Steadfast, you are,
unlike the husband and best friend
I expected at my side for life.

Not male or female, you are both.
You color the gray days of spring,
welcome bees and butterflies. And me.
Reminder to show up and grow.

—Joan Mazza

Dear Magnolia

How many days did I crouch beneath you on the damp
grass, collecting twigs and petals, shaping tiny people
and cloaking them in wilting hues of pink and rust?
A loner, I played more often by myself than with a friend,

stalking ants and beetles in the dust beneath the hedge.
Even now when magnolias flare in the yards I drive past,
creamy blossoms competing with Japanese cherry and
pear, I am back beneath you, combing the grass for clues.

If only I had not gone on a pilgrimage to the past, gone
to that remembered house my great-grandparents once
owned, hoping to see again my one true tree, or the ghost
of my young mother kneeling to weed the garden beds;

if only the new owners had not chopped you down, Magnolia,
as they chose to expand and tar the once-pebbled driveway
until all I could find of you was a blacker circle on macadam—
a black hole still devouring our crumbling roots.

—Penny Harter

Craft Tip #3: Change of Venue

—George Bilgere

About eight years ago I felt stuck. My fourth collection of poems had appeared a couple of years earlier, and my efforts to write since then had felt somehow forced and repetitive. I was working too hard to sound the way I thought, based on having written four books, I was supposed to sound. Instead of changing my *approach* to the work itself, which I really had no interest in doing, I decided to change the *way* I approached my writing.

First was a change of venue. I'd always worked in my office at home or in whatever apartment I happened to be living in at the time. Over the years, however, I'd developed the habit of reading, not writing, in cafes. Something about the buzz of activity in a café—stimulating but not too distracting—always pleased me. And somehow the unchanging silence of my office was beginning to seem burdensome. I found myself doing the things that all writers do to avoid writing: vacuuming the living room, rearranging my record albums, impulsively deciding that the bookshelves in the den absolutely had to be painted before a word of poetry could be written.

So I decided to try writing in a cozy little café down the road. I realized almost immediately it was the right choice. For one thing, looking at the people around me gave me ideas for writing I would not have had at home. And at the café there was nothing to do but write. It would look strange if I started vacuuming the floor. And it was just plain nice to not be alone, to have the hum of human activity around me. I started looking forward to my morning writing sessions in a way I hadn't for years.

I also stopped working on a computer and began writing in a notebook. I bought an artist's sketch pad, with big expanses of luxurious unlined paper. I rediscovered the pleasure of seeing my own terrible handwriting make its tentative way across the page. Watching paper absorb ink must be one of the earliest delights of writing, and it was a joy to return to it. The movement of thought from brain to arm to wrist to hand to the tip of the pen: magical.

The last change was the most fun. After I'd handwritten the first draft of the poem, I would go home and type it out on the computer. I'd let it sit there for the afternoon, then I'd have a look at it again and make whatever changes I thought might help. In the past I would wait until the weekend, take the five or six drafts of poems I'd written that week, and show them to my wife after dinner. I decided to change that to a daily event. After dinner each night I'd ask her to read the poem I'd worked on that morning. She's a terrific critic of my work, absolutely honest and very tough when necessary. I found I was looking forward all day to our little post-dinner discussion. Putting the poem under scrutiny after we'd finished our pork chops or spaghetti or salad nicoise was a wonderful little punctuation point to the day, usually accompanied by a second glass of Chardonnay. What a nice way to end an evening together, even if it meant I had to return the favor by doing the dishes.

Poem and Prompt

Box of Butterflies

Swallowtails: Tiger, Spicebush, Pipevine, and the rare Giant: gliding
      Grand Prize chased by flailing boys.
Cloudless Sulfur: yellow as a playschool sun; no whiff of hell on you.

Skipper: managing brilliantly the meadow's baseball team.
Gulf Fritillary: We sons of World War called you *Golf Artillery*.

Crescentspot: a careless painter dripped white on your orange-and-
      umber gown.
Eyed Brown: small, drab, flitting grass-high; almost too common to
      collect, then; scarce on my old street as I am, now.

Monarch: orange-and-black Majesty to which I bowed, seeing you flap,
      frantic, then sink onto my killing jar's drenched throne.
Viceroy: disguised as a Monarch to discourage birds; pretender to a
      crown for which you died, unrecognized.

Buckeye: six purple irises pining, like my mom, for Ohio.
Mourning Cloak: I spelled it *Morning*—too new to death-dealing to know.

—Charles Harper Webb

In this unusual list poem the speaker catalogs the butterflies he collected as a boy. Note the structural plan. The poem itself becomes a butterfly collection as the poet begins each line with the name of a butterfly. He follows each name with a colon and adds details, often using direct address to the butterfly and including a metaphor or two.

Stanzas are determined by the number of butterflies—two per stanza. If the description exceeds one line, the excess becomes an indented line.

Webb arranges the butterflies climactically. As he moves towards the close, the poem becomes more than a list poem, more than a poem about a boy and his butterfly collection. It becomes a poem about a boy learning what death is, what killing is. There is subtle preparation for this ending—the early *whiff of hell* and the *sons of World War*, the early misspelling of *Fritillary* as *Artillery*, and the ominous *killing jar's drenched throne*.

Be sure to read this poem aloud and listen for the delicious sounds it makes. Webb relies on the musical effects of assonance. For example, there are five long *i* sounds in just the first line: *Tiger, Spicebush, Pipevine*, and *Giant gliding*. Webb also sprinkles the poem with consonant sounds. Notice, for example, the abundance of *s* sounds in the first stanza: *Swallowtails, Spicebush, chased, boys, Cloudless Sulfur*, and *playschool sun*.

Let's take on the challenge of a list poem. Choose a category that contains numerous items, e.g., types of lettuce, roses, birds common to your locale, poisonous snakes, sleep aids, shades of blue or red, mushrooms, or something you once collected.

Now brainstorm a long list of items in your category.

Select ten of the items to use in your poem. Arrange these in a climactic order. Be open to changing this order during revision.

Now begin your draft. Add descriptive details for each item. Include some direct address and some metaphors.

Don't consider your poem done until it transcends the list. Keep adding descriptive details and metaphors until some heft emerges. You will feel the tug when that happens.

Revise for sounds. Get in a generous amount of assonance and consonance.

Sample Poems

Bird Watching

Cliff swallow: blue hat, red bandana around your neck,
      rodeo-rider of the air.
Violet-green swallow: you shimmer like a hummingbird.

American three-toed woodpecker: splash of yellow
      on your head like paint
      dripped from the high branches.
Northern flicker: flash of red beneath your wings, but only
      when you fly.

Yellow warbler: messenger of happiness skimming low
      across the water.
Western tanager: nape red like a head-wound,
      like a slit throat.

Mountain bluebird: in nature, too, blue is for boys.
Pine grosbeak: finch of the high mountain in all the shades
      of sunset.

Brewer's blackbird: common blackbird of open country
      in your simple preacher's suit.
Red-winged blackbird: falling upward.

—Jennifer Saunders

A Casino Bestiary

Wolverine triplets zing a match but one zags away.
Add dollars and shake hands with chrome handles.
Two yellow coyotes snarl and curl tails. Spin again.

A shaggy elk bull rises but stumbles downstream.
Add quarters and hear silver waterfalls tinkle.
Three rabbits disappear and appear and disappear.

Jaguar has a cameo role and departs grinning.
Add dimes and hear Wheel of Fortune ding-dong-ding.
Three honking geese fly in a line then falter.

White-tailed deer leap one after another after another.
Add buffalo nickels, buffalo nickels, buffalo nickels.
Prairie dogs on the screen swivel. Watch them vanish.

—Denise Low
published in *New Letters*

The Poet on the Poem: Lee Upton

The Clues

The woven reeds, the slats
in the middle of the path—
with the book bag, the shoe,
the empty basket.

Then, the mixed prints in the woods.
Hair shredded on a bush.
Fibers, red and black.
So much for forensics to do,

it wasn't until well past two
that we found our way
to the end of the path.
There in a cottage

rocked the girl and her family,
sipping tea. Just over their heads
a wolf pelt rippled,
the eyes spinning

in the skinned skull
regarding that domestic economy.
Three generations:
the mother, once out of the story,

now back, with her own daughter,
plus her own mother,
plus two baskets of snacks.
And all of them—that girl and those women—

brimming with so much liberty
none of them even bothered
to turn to the wall and gloat
at that patch of furry kitsch:

Just look at us,
you son of a bitch.

DL: Your poem puts a new spin on the old tale of "Little Red Riding Hood." Tell us about the inspiration for this new version. Why a detective story? What is the role of Red Riding Hood's mother in your poem?

LU: Fairy tales are so incredibly long-lived and mystery-filled that I find myself attracted to drawing from them when I write. "The Clues" invokes the plot elements of "Little Red Riding Hood" and attempts a transformation of the version of the story that I know best. I wanted to re-imagine the story, allowing the child to save herself and triumph—without the woodcutter. Here the clues lead to a vision of survival, although there is a murder of sorts: the wolf has been skinned, his pelt pegged to the wall. It's not enough, by the way, for the girl and her mother and grandmother to skin the wolf; they keep the pelt in view and as such display their own capacity for violence.

"The Clues" speaks—even if with an attempt at humor—to a common wish: to defend one's self and those we love. At the end of the poem, the detectives come upon the unexpected: three generations of women, untraumatized, celebrating their victory.

Like any parent, the mother must at some point send her child into the world, with warnings, and the child, like many children, defies those warnings.

DL: I noticed the predominance of soft *i* sounds. That vowel sound appears in every stanza, usually multiple times. In stanza 1 there's *in, middle,* and *with*; in stanza 2 there's *mixed, prints, in, forensics.* How consciously was this music crafted? What do you think it adds to the poem?

LU: I didn't think about that specific form of assonance as I wrote, but I realize now—because of your question—that those sounds ushered me to the final word of the poem, and the little explosion of triumph and disgust and joy that occurs there.

I was aware of how insistent sound repetitions were as I wrote the poem, and I did read the poem aloud after I wrote the first draft. Repetitions drew the poem forward and determined my choices. Most of the poem—its central drama and many of the sound effects—appeared in the initial draft. That's highly unusual for me; I tend to write many drafts. Subsequent drafts for this poem amounted to adjustments more than full-scale revisions.

DL: I like how you scatter rhymes throughout the poem. The *shoe* at the end of stanza 1's line 3 rhymes with *to do* at the end of stanza 2 and with *two* at the end of stanza 3. The *sipping* of stanza 4 is echoed in *rippled.* The s*pinning* that ends stanza 4 is echoed in stanza 5's *skinned* and stanza 7's *brimming.* Then there's my favorite: stanza 7's *patch* and *kitsch* rhyme so forcefully with the poem's last word, *bitch.* Tell us how you managed these rhymes. Also, ending the poem with a common curse strikes me as a risk, but one that works here. What do you think makes it work? Is it the rhyme?

LU: The insistent rhyming and assonance underscore for me the poem's allegiance to the sonic qualities of fairy tales and nursery rhymes, the way repetitive sounds may, depending on context, create an uneasy but almost rollicking atmosphere.

As for that final line: it gave me such happiness. I suppose *bitch* is a word that is problematic; I'm not reclaiming it here. The word is used in a defiant, raw way, as a reminder of the power that the girl and the women have claimed for themselves.

It's difficult not to be preoccupied with violence. A portion of an earlier poem of mine, "Clairvoyance," reflects on vulnerability and violence—with a different outcome than in "The Clues":

Fog comes under a door. No.
It's not fog, it's smoke.
It's churning, it's water.
The noise is on the other side
of a wall, high in the wall.
Now the sound is off.
And then I realize:
I am inside a dream.
A woman is being beaten.
I can reach my hand out
and the world parts.
The dream is nowhere
but the woman is
in every part of the world.

Violence is familiar to us all, and maybe a great many of us live our lives like investigators who expect patterns to be replicated. But the investigative team's expectation is upended in "The Clues." The evidence would seem to lead to the discovery of a human corpse. But those clues, for once, have been misread.

DL: Your use of point of view is effective. The poem seemingly begins in objective third person, but in stanza 3 *we* emerges, the first person plural. This voice is that of the investigative team. The last stanza appears to be the words of the three women speaking as one voice. Tell us about these shifts.

LU: With those final words we're inhabiting the investigative team members' minds—their own view of the three females' perspectives—and the unspoken view of those three females. The girl and her mother and grandmother could have said those final words but *none of them even bothered / to turn to the wall and gloat.* Their disdain allows them to focus on pleasure and to save their words for one another.

The poem emerges from a collective voice, but those final two lines break through the surface of that more distanced, puzzled, fact-bearing voice, and allow us into the minds of the women.

DL: I'm intrigued by the tone of the poem. It's mysterious and exciting as the clues build up. It's shocking and humorous at the end of the poem. I also sense some feminist anger there. Was the tone calculated or did it evolve and change organically?

LU: As soon as the final two lines arrived, they surprised me. I believed then the poem was alive—as if those lines ran backward and up through the poem and re-lit all previous lines. The women are brimming with energy, as full human beings not to be tampered with or condescended to. The wolf's eyes are *spinning* at their boldness; we're in the world of fairy tales where such things can happen. But if the skinned pelt is a reminder of the courage and cunning of generations of women, the wolf's living eyes suggest that the wolf is never entirely destroyed.

Bonus Prompt: Morning Poem

You are going to write a morning poem of twelve or more lines.

Include one or more lines about each of the following items in this order:

1. something you saw this morning

2. something you smelled

3. something you tasted

4. something you saw

5. something you felt

6. something you heard

7. something you saw

8. something you tasted

9. something you remembered

10. something you wanted

11. something you saw

12. a statement about the morning

Now go through the draft and insert two negative statements anywhere you want them. These lines might begin with such phrases as *I did not, There was no*, or *I could not.*

Shake up the poem by rearranging the order of the lines.

Cut out what isn't working.

Note: If you're writing at night, feel free to make this a night poem. Adjust the directions accordingly.

II. Entryways into Poems

The poet is a liar who always speaks the truth.

—Jean Cocteau

Craft Tip #4: Portals into Poems

—Sheryl St. Germain

We focus a lot in creative writing pedagogy on how to build a poem. Little is written about how to find the materials that create an opening to the poem. A lot of soul-work goes into finding those materials.

When I was a young poet, I had the luck to study with the poet Galway Kinnell. I once asked him a complicated question about form and technique in poetry. He listened patiently, then said, *Just say what the truth is, Sheryl.* I have never forgotten his advice, which is both simple and deep in the way that Zen koans sometimes are.

Truth, however one defines it, is not easy. It may be that you need to reach for an emotional truth or a metaphorical truth, not the literal truth. Perhaps it's a truth that acknowledges an ambivalence about something you thought you felt one way or another about, or perhaps it's a truth you fear no one will like. That recognition is the entrance to the poem.

After my conversation with Galway those many years ago, I retired to my room and wrote a poem called "Addiction," about my brother's drug overdose and my own participation in it. It starts like this:

> The truth is I loved it,
> the whole ritual of it,
> the way he would fist up his arm, then
> hold it out so trusting and bare,
> the vein pushed up all blue and throbbing
> and wanting to be pierced...

and ends like this:

> When I think of my brother
> all spilled out on the floor

I say nothing to anyone.
I know what it's like to want joy
at any cost.

This excerpt is from the poem of mine that is most anthologized and perhaps, for better or worse, the poem for which I am most known. It is the poem I am most content with having written. Without Galway's admonition to say what the truth is, I might never have written this poem. Once I got the first line, the rest of the poem almost wrote itself. It was as if I had hit a metaphorical vein, something that had been waiting to be tapped, and it all came tumbling out. Because I had had a sufficient training in technique, I was able to feel my way through the decisions that needed to be made regarding form.

Most good poems begin with a kind of listening to the soul's music. If the word *soul* bothers you, think of the music of the psyche or the spirit. When we are constantly distracted by email, social media, the demands of work and family, it is difficult to find a space where you can actively listen to the rich silence inside you. But you must in order to find portals to truths, doors to poems that will matter.

So my first advice to those who would be poets is to find a place truly free of distractions where you can do some deep listening, any quiet place where you do not have your cell phone, access to social media, or email for a time.

What is the truth you never say? Is there something your mother (father, lover, spouse) wishes you wouldn't say? Something your culture wishes you wouldn't say? Say it. Begin a poem with *The truth is,* and see where it leads you, or take one of your poems that is not working for some reason and ask of it what truth it might be ignoring or what truth it has failed to articulate, and perhaps your poem will begin to breathe.

Poem and Prompt

Lesson

At some location between the rod itself
and the hook, which, having shot straight
on its filament through the locust-sung
summer air (all sun-blistered
and clover-hung), at the flick
of her cousin's right wrist until it reached
the soft crease of her inner elbow, where
it snagged and he laughed (she cried out)—
that tender purchase of dart in flesh
allowing him to reel her bleating back
along a taut line of rancid animal pain
she couldn't unfasten from—at some
point along that axis humming casual
violence (and his boy heat and her blood
just beginning to bubble under the barb),
a false idea she had about this world
and her position in it was corrected.

—Karin Gottshall

So much gets accomplished in this short poem—and in just one sentence. Gottshall presents us with two young people on the threshold between innocence and experience, a threshold that gets crossed not when the boy lands a fish hook in the girl's arm, but when he laughs about it.

The poet uses a third person speaker which seems essential and just right for this poem. A first person speaker, the boy or the girl, could not objectively or convincingly draw the conclusion that a third person speaker can.

Notice the parentheses which occur three times. These break the flow of the sentence and cause us to pause a bit. They allow the speaker to add information and still maintain the single sentence structure. The dashes function in the same way.

Notice, also, the fanciful use of compound words, invented by joining a noun and a past participle with a hyphen: *locust-sung* and *sun-blistered* and *clover-hung*. The lovely vowel sounds here are scattered throughout the poem. They are echoed later in *from*, *some*, and *humming*. The rhymes and the assonance of such soft musical sounds make a nice contrast to the hard consonant *b* sounds of *boy*, *blood*, *beginning*, *bubble*, and *barb*.

For your own poem, choose an incident that involved two people—one could be you or someone like you—both in a state of innocence. They might be but do not need to be as young as Gottshall's characters. Let something happen that changes one or both of the characters, e.g., an act of animal cruelty, vandalism, bullying, theft. One character hurts, betrays, or disappoints the other in some way.

Use third person, but put the wounded person in the spotlight. Without letting the poem become overly or overtly didactic, hint at some kind of conclusion, some suggestion that one of the characters is changed by the experience.

Create some compound words by combining noun and past participle.

Experiment with the use of parentheses and dashes. Keep what works. Abandon what doesn't.

Get in some vowel rhymes, i.e., some assonance. Try to contrast the soft sounds with some hard ones.

As you draft and revise, strive for a single sentence which pulls together all elements of the incident.

Sample Poems

Timmy Kickboxing at Age Seven

Oiled in sweat,
red marks blooming on his pale torso,
Timmy kicks at Brian's navel,

but when Brian's leg flies up,
it's a brick flying
into his face.

Over and over Brian's kicks
—aimed at his chest—
launch into his cheeks,

his teeth wobbling.
He refuses to show
he's wounded.

His legs flail at odd angles,
like a camel's, but they don't
carry the fist-quick punch

of Brian's. Finally the brawl ends,
his face—flushed,
indignant, angry.

He and Brian bow to each other
like old war horses
dipping their heads.

—Bob Bradshaw

Her Father's Nose

As multiple hands pummeled the basketball, stealing it,
slap-swish—swerving back and forth, kid-stretched arms
shooting at the netless hoop on the school playground—
her feet skittering on the concrete-rough court,
one of the knee-scabbed girls slammed into her, a ball-slip—
get out of my way, you hooked-nose Mexican.
The taunt face-slapped her red, seared her through.
Later, turned sideways in the mirror, realizing she
had indeed inherited her father's nose and more—
her world shifted, how she must zigzag through it.

—Gloria Amescua

Craft Tip #5: Including Laughter: Techniques for Using Humor in Poetry

—Kelli Russell Agodon

I use humor in my poems as a backdoor into topics that are difficult to write about. When my father died three months after my college graduation, I realized that if I could ever laugh again, I would be okay. My father, who had a wicked sense of humor, lives through many of the poems I've written about him. By using humor to deal with his death, I feel as if I've succeeded in keeping his memory alive.

Humor acknowledges that hope exists. When I use my poems to laugh at my demons and poke fun at them, I gain the upper hand over them.

But how to write a humorous poem? There is no one particular subject appropriate for humorous poems, nor is there just one way to write a funny poem. In fact, there are several ways to add humor and surprise to a poem, but the four techniques I use and appreciate most are *wordplay, exaggeration, repetition,* and *line breaks.*

1. Wordplay
Whether I'm writing an *anagram* poem where I'm respelling *funeral* and turning it into *real fun* or changing *death and poetry* into *donated therapy,* finding words inside other words creates humor through discovery. The element of surprise in anagram poems produces joy despite the poem's topic.

A *mondegreen*, which is a misheard phrase or lyric, can open the door to laughter or absurdity in poems. I have an entire poem created from the phrase *how killer blue irises spread* because I misheard a news report on NPR. The real newscast spoke of how killer *flu viruses* spread, but that was not what I heard. That error opened the door into a poem topic I would not have stumbled upon on my own. I used the misheard news report as the title and then took the reader into a made-up world of murderous plants.

The *portmanteau*, literally a suitcase with two compartments, is another type of wordplay. This literary term was first used by Lewis Carroll to describe taking parts of two different words and putting them together to make one new word. For example, Carroll created the word *slithy* for his poem "Jabberwocky" by blending the words *lithe* and *slimy*. Invented words offer readers surprise and the satisfaction of deciphering the two words used.

2. Exaggeration

This tool of overemphasizing and stretching what is said should also be in every poet's toolbox. Here's how Nin Andrews begins her prose poem "Yes": *Orgasms are bad news. In the town where I grew up, orgasms were against the law. No one had an orgasm, not even God. By the time I was twelve, I wanted an orgasm. Just one, I begged.* Clearly, the poet is exaggerating rather than being factual and exact. By the end of the poem, the story has become larger than life: *The people were outraged. They chased me into the streets and out of the city gates...With these orgasms that never stop singing my name.* Andrews' use of exaggeration creates a unique tension and keeps us wanting to know what will happen next.

Such poems can produce humor by pushing both poet and reader to stretch their limits. Exaggeration allows the poet to turn ordinary details into extraordinary ones, to juxtapose silliness with reality, playfulness with seriousness.

3. Repetition

Recently I participated in a group reading of Gertrude Stein's *Tender Buttons,* a collection in which even the repetition is repetitive. While the poems were being read aloud, the group began to laugh as words and phrases were repeated, as in the poem, "Mildred's Umbrella":

> A cause and no curve, a cause and loud enough, a cause and extra a loud clash and an extra wagon, a sign of extra, a sac a small sac and an established color and cunning, a slender grey and no ribbon, this means a loss a great loss a restitution.

Stein repeats not only words, but also sounds with her use of assonance and consonance. Repetition creates humor and music and offers the reader the pleasure of the nonsensical.

Take a phrase, a word, an image, an idea, and repeat it in your poem—it creates a touchstone for the reader and a sense of play. Sprinkle with a little wonder and ridiculousness, and watch the poem snowball.

4. Line breaks

A line broken at the ideal spot during a distressing scene can add surprise and wit to a poem, offering a moment to breathe, a smile of relief, or maybe even a laugh. For example, consider reading a poem about someone very ill in a hospital and coming to this line:

> In the hospital room, he was dying

That's worrisome. But now imagine coming to these two lines:

> In the hospital room, he was dying
> for ice cream...

We're left with a lighter feeling and a moment of recovery, whether or not the poem continues in a more humorous tone or moves into sorrowful territory.

Marvin Bell has a poem about his wife called "To Dorothy." His first line makes his readers gasp; it begins, *You are not beautiful, exactly*. We are left wondering where this poem is going and did the poet just call his wife unattractive? But the second line continues, *You are beautiful, inexactly*, and the same readers relax and smile.

Allow humor to open doors into topics you're having trouble with and don't be afraid to mix humor with sadder moments in the poem. Isn't this what life is? The good mixed with the bad: the most beautiful day of the year, a promotion at work, and a funeral? Our world is a mix of the comical and the sorrowful— and sometimes at the same time. By acknowledging both, your work can achieve a new complexity.

Poem and Prompt

Lockdown

We went into lockdown last week as a madwoman terrorized
the city. But I was not afraid even for a second. I read from
my book of prayers, which always helps get me what I want.
A house so enormous that I have bad dreams about the impossibility
of filling it with enough furniture. A house too grandiose for a party
of humble souls who want only to smoke pot in the garage
or maybe sit on the deck observing the local catbirds. There
are prayers that take me to lunch with you in the train station
in the past and that involve my eating baked Alaska for the first
time. I avoid the prayers of erotic longing. Even if they are answered,
it simply means new longings are right around the corner. I do not
pray for rain, for I hate rain, as is well-known. I pray that "before" will
always come before "after." I pray that now will continue to precede
later, though I recognize that all of these concepts are just words,
not realities. I pray for words to become realities. I pray for one of those
cars that drives and parks itself, as I am not good at those skills
on my own. I pray that my hammer stops thinking everything
is a nail. I pray that it will rain in foreign words of desire.

—Terence Winch

I admire the way Winch mixes the serious with the humorous. His speaker tells us about a terrifying lockdown, but then adds that he was not afraid because he had his book of prayers. He says that this book *always helps get me what I want,* making us wonder just how devout his prayers are. He lists the various items he's prayed for, some serious, some frivolous. Most of the items get details. Some do not. After listing several items, the speaker switches to the negative, that is, to what he does not pray for. Just as a pattern seems to have been established, this unexpected twist adds surprise.

In line 8 an auditor emerges, addressed as *you* but never again referred to, never identified. We are left to wonder who is being addressed.

In the second half of the poem, the poet makes effective use of anaphora, setting up a rhythmic chant with the repetition of *I pray*. This has the effect of giving the poem steam and increasing power as it moves toward its close.

Notice the stunning metaphor that appears in the penultimate line and notice the skillful line break there: *I pray that my hammer stops thinking everything / is a nail*. Finally, notice how the last line pulls together three items that appeared earlier in the poem: *rain, words,* and *desire.*

For your own prayer poem, first come up with a situation that might warrant some prayers. This might be something drawn from the news or from your own life. Instead of prayers, you might think of wishes, wants, or desires.

Brainstorm a quick list of the unusual items your speaker might pray for. Add to this a few things your speaker would not pray for. Mingle the serious and the frivolous.

Now begin your draft. Draw from your brainstorming list and follow Winch's pattern of positive—negative—positive.

As you continue drafting, add details to several of the items.

Employ anaphora in the second half of your draft.

Imagine an auditor and refer to him/her just once—or perhaps not at all. Even just imagining an auditor will add voice to your poem.

As you approach what feels like the end of your poem, move to the metaphorical. End with a final prayer that pulls together three of the earlier prayers. This will almost surely result in a line that surprises you.

Sample Poems

Turbulence

Last week the Airbus flying me across the ocean
hit turbulence and suddenly dropped. My book
flew up from my hands, my water
spilled across my lap and my lap strained at my seatbelt
but I was not afraid. I carry a list of prayers in my head
so I prayed for a lawn so perfect
it could be mistaken for a golf course.
A rose bush that never needs pruning.
I prayed for deer to come to my yard
but not to nibble on the Japanese maple.
I prayed for a bird feeder
that keeps out the squirrels,
for I do not like the sound of squirrels
as they run up and around the oak tree.
I prayed for a pair of orioles
to visit the feeder each morning
and for you to stand beside me at the window
as they rise and fly away.
I did not pray for wind. I did not pray for time
to stand still, not even the time
you stand beside me at the window.
I pray the horizon will stop marching closer
and I pray the wind will blow a lock of your hair
into my perfect yard.

—Jennifer Saunders

Prayers for the Victims

I wish them trumpets and marching bands,
marionettes, and manicured parks and wilderness
to wander in, and bears that purr instead of bite.
I wish them warm blankets, not cold hands,
their favorite ice cream flavors, not school lunches.
I wish them umbrellas that carry themselves,
bandages that heal while holding. I wish them
good sex, and no police interviews.
I wish them coffee in the morning, and lollipops,
and tongues that wash away wounds, caress slurs
into sweet talk, sweet cocoa. I wish them
mountain lakes, or oceans, as they prefer,
and no tornadoes or other frightening weather.
I wish them unconditional love, the kind
you give me. May it be shelter. May it
smooth them. May it render them whole.

—Lisken Van Pelt Dus

Craft Tip #6: Are Your Titles Like Limp Handshakes?

—Martha Silano

Every poem's title is like a handshake, your first chance at making a strong impression. An editor friend often confides in me about poems that cross her desk titled "Rain" and "Insect." Poems with bland and uninspiring titles like these just don't demand to be read. Not one bit. But a poem with a title like "The Gargantuan Muffin Beauty Contest"—who could resist?

Here are a few ideas for how to extend a hand to your reader that he or she will definitely want to shake:

1. Create a title that will be repeated, in part or in whole, in the first line of the poem.

My curiosity is piqued by a title like Theodore Roethke's "I Knew a Woman," a title that makes us wonder what's special about that woman and why the past tense is used. Is there a story to be told? The title then gets repeated and expanded in the first line: *I knew a woman, lovely in her bones /...*" The poet rewards our curiosity as the rest of the poem lives up to the allure of its grabber title.

Wyn Cooper's "Chaos is the New Calm" functions similarly, allowing the speaker to get right to the meat and potatoes, serving up, in the first and second lines, *Chaos is the new calm / violence the new balm* and closing with this pirouetting couplet: *Don't strand me standing here. / If you leave, leave beer.*

Caution: Don't overuse this technique. If you use it in poem after poem, your readers will get wise to you and stop reading the first line. Use this technique only if the title bears repeating.

2. Create a title that serves as the first line or first word of the poem.

When done well, the title's enticement to keep reading pays off in spades. Note how Eduardo Corral's title grabs our attention and then runs right into the poem, functioning as its first line:

In Colorado My Father Scoured and Stacked Dishes

> in a Tex-Mex restaurant. His co-workers,
> unable to utter his name, renamed him Jalapeño.

The title of Bob Hicok's poem "Thought" serves as the first word of the first line: *of Job when her friend died...*

This title technique creates speed by eliminating the usual pause between title and first line.

3. Let the title introduce a word or phrase reiterated in the body of the poem.

In David Rivard's "Otherwise Elsewhere" both words of the title are repeated multiple times throughout the poem. The two words are then collapsed into *elsewise* which is also repeated several times. The title thus introduces the music and wordplay of the poem.

After grabbing our attention with his title, "The Gargantuan Muffin Beauty Contest," Julian Stannard then weaves the word *muffin* throughout his poem. Each time the word is repeated, it gathers steam:

> I've never seen so many high-quality muffins.
> If I wasn't a religious man, and maybe I wasn't
> I would have said the muffins were walking on water:
> I've never felt so half-and-half. Have you read the Bible?
> The bellhop said: You ain't seen muffin yet.

4. Incorporate the name of the poem's form into the title.

You might want to do this if your readers are possibly unfamiliar with the form, but it can be kind of boring, so to spice things up try rhyming or riffing off the form's name.

Consider Mark Jarman's "Unholy Sonnet 1." I don't know about you, but I'm more likely to read a sonnet if I know from the get-go that it's going to be unholy. Kathy Fagan's "Saloon Pantoum" and Doug Lang's "Tina Sestina" pull me in with their rhyming titles which offer up nice music and provide a little crucial information about the pantoum or sestina I'm about to commit my time to.

5. Create a title that provides essential background information.

Such a title can pave the way for *in medias res* beginnings and pre-emptively clarify what's going on in the poem. These opening lines by David Wagoner might leave the reader confused about what's going on: *I've watched his eyelids sag, spring open / Vaguely and gradually go sliding / Shut again, fly up.* But the poet anticipates and kills the confusion with his title, "For a Student Sleeping in a Poetry Workshop." By the time we get to the eyelids in the first line, we already know that they belong to a student. We can now picture the situation.

Same goes with Paisley Rekdal's title, "Mae West: Advice." Without that title, we'd have no idea who was giving the advice, making the poem way less fun.

6. Create a title that contains details that might be cumbersome in the poem.

Beginning writers sometimes have this notion in their heads that they can't use their titles to explain crucial details about the poem, such as the setting or the impetus for the poem. Simply adding a bit more detail to your title may very well encourage your reader to read on and, at the same time, result in a tighter and often more lyrical poem. Instead of "Rain," how about "My Cat Does Not Like the Rain"? Instead of "Peaches," Wallace Stevens wisely titled his poem "A Dish of Peaches in Russia." Such a title is an efficient way of providing information.

7. Use a title to add mystery or provoke curiosity, the quirkier and more enticing, the better.

Who could resist reading Kerrin McCadden's "If You Were a Zombie Boy," Marcus Wicker's "Creation Song in Which a Swift Wind Sucker Punches a Transformer," Cynthia Marie Hoffman's "The Calciferous Substance Speaks to the Sleeping Fetus," or Dafydd Wood's "The Graduate Student in Comparative Literature Weighs the Merits of a Career in Pornographic Film"?

I think you get my drift; such seductively zany titles demand our attention.

Which of these approaches to titling will work best depends, of course, on the poem. Err on the side of the unusual, if not a little bit strange, and at least you won't run the risk of making an editor or reader snore.

Poem and Prompt

Abecedarian Requiring Further Examination of Anglikan Seraphym Subjugation of a Wild Indian Rezervation

Angels don't come to the reservation.
Bats, maybe, or owls, boxy mottled things.
Coyotes, too. They all mean the same thing—
death. And death
eats angels, I guess, because I haven't seen an angel
fly through this valley ever.
Gabriel? Never heard of him. Know a guy named Gabe though—
he came through here one powwow and stayed, typical
Indian. Sure he had wings,
jailbird that he was. He flies around in stolen cars. Wherever he stops,
kids grow like gourds from women's bellies.
Like I said, no Indian I've ever heard of has ever been or seen an angel.
Maybe in a Christmas pageant or something—
Nazarene church holds one every December,
organized by Pastor John's wife. It's no wonder
Pastor John's son is the angel—everyone knows angels are white.
Quit bothering with angels, I say. They're no good for Indians.
Remember what happened last time
some white god came floating across the ocean?
Truth is, there may be angels, but if there are angels
up there, living on clouds or sitting on thrones across the sea wearing
velvet robes and golden rings, drinking whiskey from silver cups,
we're better off if they stay rich and fat and ugly and
'xactly where they are—in their own distant heavens.
You better hope you never see angels on the rez. If you do, they'll be
        marching you off to
Zion or Oklahoma, or some other hell they've mapped out for us.

—Natalie Diaz

As the title indicates, this poem is written in the form known as an *abecedarian*. While Diaz includes all twenty-six letters of the alphabet in her title, that's not a requirement of the form. The one rule is that each line must begin with a letter of the alphabet, starting with *A* and going through *Z*, resulting in a poem of twenty-six lines. There are no rules regarding topic, line lengths, stanzas, rhyming, or meter. Line lengths and breaks are dictated by the letter needed to begin the next line's first word. Thus, this form offers a good mixture of restriction and freedom.

Diaz addresses a serious topic—angels on the Indian reservation. But she adds touches of humor: *Sure he had wings, / jailbird that he was.* Then her humor turns serious: *Wherever he stops, / kids grow like gourds from women's bellies.*

The poem has a strong voice. The first person speaker talks to someone living on the reservation and doesn't sugarcoat what she sees as the truth: *Angels don't come to the reservation. / Bats, maybe, or owls, boxy mottled things. / Coyotes, too. They all mean the same thing— / death.* The diction is colloquial and direct: *Like I said* and *Quit bothering with angels, I say. They're no good for Indians.* The speaker asks questions and uses dashes.

For your own alphabet poem, first choose a topic, perhaps a social issue such as global warming, drugs, homelessness. Or perhaps something lighter such as mushroom foraging, planting a garden, naming the cosmos. A category topic, one with a large vocabulary, might also work: flowers, spices, diseases.

Now write the alphabet down the left side of your page and draft your poem. If you get stuck at a letter, leave that line blank and move to the next letter. Remember that the first word in a line can be any part of speech and need not be an important word.

In revision, remember that you're free to break your poem into stanzas. Get in a few metaphors. Work on voice. Let us hear a real human being speaking. Be sure your abecedarian, like Diaz's, transcends the form and is more than a mere exercise.

Give your poem an inviting title. It may or may not identify the form.

Sample Poems

At the Synapse of Memory

At fifty forgetting
began. You skipped sessions,
chased memory, rode every slope
downhill—your mind in free fall towards
embarrassment, loss,
fragmentation—yours, yet mine to mind as wife and
gifted nurse (for goodness sake), mine to
harbor hopes, chance on
impotence.
Jerked through tests, we
knew the losers
lay waste in nursing homes.

Meanwhile white lab-coats plied
neurons and synapses,
opened rat minds to scrutinize
pathogens in Alzheimer
quagmires.
Research spun promises like spiders,
strung us along with hope,
tease and trap.

Unceasing, these days—mine alone to
visit you, love—to mourn a mind
withered and warehoused,
x-ed out beyond
yearnings, always
zipped shut.

—Betsey Cullen

Before Us

all that lived
before we arrived
cries for us to bear witness
defend our planet from our pride
engage the present, decry change deniers
forgive our forbears their transgressions
grant our posterity their needful lessons
heed summons of true souls, hear stars' call
interpret fading scripts with wisdom overarching all
justify nothing, sustain justice
keep council with earth and sea
lavish our best thoughts on continuance and duty
manifest joy each day, make, do, be
nourish all sentience and harvest beauty
open blue portals of our hearts
propose peace before conflict starts
question any presumptions
resist all rote prescriptions
sustain indigenous insights
traverse unforgotten country
understand grey vagaries of our minds
value their meanderings, open their blinds
warm each cold, assist our old
xenocides unthought, banish with forethought
yet let acceptance bloom and ever onward, forward
zoom.

—Akua Lezli Hope

The Poet on the Poem: Tony Hoagland

Give Me Your Wife

because I like her. I like

the signs of wear on her;
the way her breasts have dropped a little with the years;
the weathered evidence of joy around her eyes.

I like her faded jeans,
her hennaed hair;
her hips pried open by the child.

I find her interesting; her grey-eyed
calm of a resigned sea;
her stillness like a painting on the wall.

It's not that you don't care,
but after all, you're just a man
who has been standing in

water up to his neck for years,
and never managed to quite
dunk his head entirely under.

So give me your wife. Recycle her.
Look at her mouth, like a soft dry rose;
the way she stands, at an angle

to the world.
She could still be kissed and joked with,
teased into a bed

with cool white sheets;
convinced to lie and be
laid down upon.

Happiness might
still find a place
for her.

Give me your wife
like you were
unbuttoning something
accidentally

and leaving it behind.
Then just drift away
and let me try.

DS: You begin with a 1-line stanza, followed by nine 3-line stanzas, then one 4-line stanza, and finally another 3-line stanza. What's the logic behind this stanza arrangement?

TH: My decisions are motivated by the simplest possible reasons for arrangement—pacing and content—but the poem should probably be, and mostly is, in tercets, for their processional pacing. What is happening in the poem is a kind of ceremonial asking, which needs to have a rhythmical pace.

DS: You also use inconsistent line lengths. Line 1 is just six words with a total of seven syllables. Line 4 is eleven words, twelve syllables. Line 3 juts way out into the right margin. How did you determine your line lengths and breaks?

TH: Very organically, in semantic units, with the occasional but not too difficult enjambment. I believe in the poem as immersive dream; almost all decisions, many of them anyway, are devoted to clarity, and keeping the reader effortlessly inside the poem, in the dream of the poem, which should be like a ride down a river.

DS: Your title does double duty, serving as both title and part of the sentence that's completed in the first two lines of the poem. What do you think are the benefits of this kind of title?

TH: Swiftness, quickness of immersion, and involvement. Poems that, like a horse, get out of the gate fast have a great advantage. This is especially true of what I call *relational* poems, poems that are making a direct and intimate address to the reader as well as to the addressee of the poem, if different. I don't remember exactly the first time I saw a poem's title slide straight into its first sentence, but I remember thinking, *That's a cool thing.*

DL: The poem has a distinctive voice, beginning with the bossy directive of the title. You use a first person speaker, a man who desires another man's wife. You also use direct address to an auditor, the husband of the wife. Please talk about how you intended these two choices to affect the voice and the reader's response to the speaker.

TH: I realize this positioning of speaker to the drama at hand will be off-putting to some—obviously for its presumptions about a woman or wife as a kind of property. In some of my poems, I deliberately choose a kind of initially aggressive stance as a way of making things interesting, but that is not the case in this poem.

After I wrote the poem some years ago, I showed it to one or two of my reader-friends and they were nonplussed by the premise. They were women readers, but hardly prudish persons, and so, although I liked the poem, I accepted their verdict of my obtuseness and put it away for a few years. By the time it came out of the drawer, I had forgotten it, though I still liked it when I read it again.

Nonetheless, I still believe that a poem has a greater duty towards actuality than ideological purity. Poems are not interesting for their political inoffensiveness but rather for their psychological verity, and whether we approve or not, men and women look at others as a kind of possession, often enough. If the psychological reality is there, why not write a poem that inhabits and explores such a stance and such a situation to the fullest? If the observation that the virtues of a perfectly good woman or man are wasted on their spouse is a common thought—and who has not felt this?—then why not write a poem making that argument real?

And the poem—though it *is* objectifying—is a poem of observant praise, and also a somewhat resigned critique of men and women and their relations.

DL: The tone of the poem is affected by the diction and imagery, both of which often seem in conflict with each other. For example, the speaker instructs the auditor, that is, the husband, to *Recycle* his wife. That word implies that she's a reusable item. But in the next line the speaker describes the wife's mouth as a *soft dry rose*, a delicate and appealing image though perhaps suggesting that the wife is past the bloom of youth. The wife is also described with such words as *interesting, weathered, faded,* and *resigned,* all of which make her sound over-the-hill and rather dull. But then *she could still be kissed and joked with, / teased into a bed // with cool white sheets; // convinced to lie and be / laid down upon.* These words and images make her sound desirable, though perhaps a bit credulous. Talk to us about your use of contrasting diction and imagery and the contribution they make to the poem's tone.

TH: These tunings of diction and rhetoric for me are the essence of most poems that I like—whether it is Fanny Howe's poem "My Broken Heart" or Lawrence's "Bavarian Gentians." Tone is the greatest instrument of poetry and comes from the alloy, or fusion, of contradictions in our attitudes and experience. The bloom *is* off our rose. That doesn't make us undesirable, or desire-free. In fact, a weathered body, face, consciousness can obviously be a marvelous—what shall I say?—asset? object? property? As Rilke says, we've earned our faces; or, as Galway Kinnell says, *The wages of death are love.* This poem acknowledges the existence of a kind of Eros which I hope we are all familiar with; not to be denied, but to be cherished, even if it is only in fantasy—and *that* is a whole other subject.

Bonus Prompt: The Borrowed Title Poem

Get your hands on a recent poetry journal and go through the table of contents. Select one title to work with. Using that title, write your way into a new poem. Do not use the title as your title. Instead, use it to inspire the idea for your poem, as a line in your poem, or as words scattered throughout your poem.

Here's a sample list of titles from the March 2009 issue of *Poetry*.

1. Three Six Five Zero

2. Coyote, with Mange

3. The Corn Baby

4. A Gift

5. Fox in the Landscape

6. Landscape with Horse Named Popcorn

7. What I Have

8. Leave the Hand In

III. Choosing the Right Words

Poetry is as precise as geometry.

—Gustave Flaubert

Craft Tip #7: Sound and Sense

—Michael T. Young

It is axiomatic that poets are born from a love for language and typically that love is for what we loosely call its *music*. However, language is inextricably bound up with meaning. So in whatever way a poet's language and poetics evolve, it is always toward greater integration of sound and sense. Finding the right words has as much to do with how those words resonate phonetically with each other as how much they resonate semantically with each other.

The pure joy of letting the tongue dance with its words is, for me, how the best work comes. It starts, and really ends, in that joy. I think of my children in this respect who are still young and learning language by playing with it, sometimes repeating a new word until it no longer sounds like itself or making up words to mean whatever it is inside them they don't yet have a word for, or perhaps for a feeling or thought there really isn't a word for. That is the fertile soil of all poets because we call it *word play* and not *word work*, after all. That's not to say it isn't difficult or challenging. But playfulness in the spirit of tackling linguistic problems makes finding the solutions not only easier but more likely to be good ones. It's word play that will hit upon the right ambiguity to clarify rather than muddy the waters. It's word play that will seek the dynamic connections and not merely the functional but dull ones.

Take as an example how meaning and music are united in the following line from Dean Kostos' poem "Saturnine": *The students slant telescopes toward oblivion*. The choice of the verb *slant* is unusual because in casual conversation the word any of us would have chosen is *turn*. So why not use *turn* in the poem? There are semantic reasons, of course, the obvious one being that telescopes are always tilted at an angle, they are *slanted*. But phonetically, *slant* starts with *s* and ends with *t* while the very next word *telescopes* reverses that, starting with *t* and ending with *s*. That results in a phonetic enactment of turning the telescope: the sounds of the words themselves turn. Look also at how tightly the sounds are woven through the line. *Slant* has nearly twice as many phonetic relationships to the other words than the word *turn* could have. The *r* in *turn* would connect only to *toward* and leave both *t* and *n* to connect with *students*, the *t* with *telescopes* and the *n* with *oblivion*. But the *s, t, l,* and *n* sounds in *slant* tie in with all the other major words of the line more intimately, sharing three of those sounds with *students* and *telescopes*, and two with *oblivion*.

When writing a poem, let the sound of the words guide your choices. Pick a word you like for its sound as your subject, title, or beginning word. Perhaps make it a word you don't even know the definition of yet. Of course, look it up. But whatever you do, let the pleasure of the sounds, the music, surprise you as you hit upon unusual associations. Allow not only internal rhymes, but consonance, assonance, and slant rhyme to suggest the next words. Taste their textures on your tongue as palatably as a fresh peach or perfectly seared filet mignon. Once you have your poem, look at those particular choices, see if and how they deepen the meaning of the poem. If they are lost on you, see if there are better choices, but if they guide you somewhere unexpected and meaningful, keep it and maybe even begin drafts that follow those other associations further.

Alternatively, take a poem that's just not working. Read through it, noting words to change, most especially the verbs. Choose some different verbs paying particular attention to the sound of the words chosen and how they resonate with the words nearby or even two or three lines away. Let that music and association guide you in fresh directions, careful not to turn it too quickly back to dictionary definitions. There's enough time for that later, once you have something that makes you taste the words in your mouth and want to recite them to the rafters even if no one else is in the room.

Poem and Prompt

Deer

They hang her in the barn, head down, tongue fat,
      dripping blood. I am left alone
      for a moment, venture close to stroke dark fur
      made rough by winter; that is when she is whole,
      intact before butchering. I'm not sure
      if they shot her, or hit her by accident
      with the truck, but she comes from the mountains
      out of season so it is the darkness that counts, not
      how she died. All winter long we'll eat her
      in secret: steaks, stews, bones boiled for broth
      and the dogs. But what I will remember is
      the rough way men's hands turn back the hide, jerk
      down hard to tear it off her body. A dull hunting
      knife cracks and disjoints the carcass.
      Dismembers it piece by piece.
      The hide disappears—left untanned, taken
      to the dump. For years afterward I walk
      out to the barn, scrape my foot against
      the stained floor beneath the crossbeam,
      never tell anyone
                    I've been taken like that.

—Deborah Miranda

Miranda describes in detail the gutting and skinning of a deer. As the deer has been caught out of season, there is an element of the clandestine here. The first person speaker, a woman, observes the men who do the action; thus, there is a feeling of objective distancing—that is, until the end of the poem which stuns us with its simplicity and its brutality, even though the speaker does not specify how she has *been taken like that*.

This poem illustrates that free verse does not mean that attention to form and music are ignored. Note, for example, the strategic use of indentation after the first line so that the entire poem hangs from that first line. Then notice the use of a dropped line at the end to suspend the telling of the secret.

The poem is written in a series of declarative sentences with just one fragment. The sentences add to the tone of cold objectivity. This tone makes the ending of the poem all the more powerful. Although it becomes clear that the event occurred in the past, the poem is written in present tense which gives it immediacy and turns us into witnesses.

Notice the hard sounds that dominate throughout the poem—the b sound in *barn, blood, by, before butchering*; the p in *dripping, piece by piece, disappears, dump, scrape*; the k in *stroke dark, truck, darkness, steaks, back, jerk*; and the t in *tongue, fat, left, moment, hit, truck*. These sounds are perfect for the hard subject matter.

For your poem, choose a dramatic action to describe. Let it be something dark, even brutal, e.g., a car accident, a dog fight, a snake swallowing a rodent, a cat stalking a bird.

Use first person and present tense. Let your speaker observe but not participate. Then bring it on home with a stark revelation at the end.

As you write the descriptive part, move your draft into metaphor. Ask yourself, What is this like? What happened to me or someone I know that was like this action? It might take you days to arrive at the metaphor part. Or, if you're lucky, it might come to you as a gift.

As you revise your draft, pay careful attention to sounds. Which sounds dominate? Can you exploit them a bit? Are they the right sounds? Do they convey some understated repressed passion? Make diction changes to get better sounds. Let the sounds echo the sense of the poem.

Sample Poems

Sisterhood

Brakes lock. A car screeches to a stop. A door opens, a woman darts out, almost falls, begins to run, sandals sliding, slipping in the gravel-coated strip beside the road. A man leaps from the driver's seat, leaves the car cantilevered in the street and runs her down. On my porch I huddle, mute. He grabs her hair, spins her around. His fist shoots out. She sags, a rag doll kept on her feet by his hand in her hair. I don't yell at him to stop, or threaten to call the police. No, I sit frozen, afraid to move as he drags her back to the car, pushes her inside, and fishtails away. What I remember is the silence as the violence unfolded, how not once did the woman cry out. She knew how this would end, knew as I did—no one listens to our screams.

—Judith Quaempts
published in *Camroc Press Review*

Under the Beech Tree

A piercing sound rattled my ear, the wind
blew through trees. I peered into the woods,
the forest froze like hands on a broken clock.

An alien utterance, part shriek part scream.
My eyes fixed on a quickened shadow where
a few berries and acorns scattered—

a blue object wrestled to the ground.
Inching closer I noticed the lifeless clump,
the crackle of leaves beneath my feet, an invisible

critter whisked through pachysandra covering.
From the bough of the beech tree,
the forest watchdog called *thief, thief, thief.*

Like a torn piece of denim, the dead bird lay there,
plucked feathers, purple crest, ripples on wings,
her strong bill, the color of charcoal.

Birds circled the battle site. The one on the branch
ranted a few more times and flew away. Even years later,

I never tell anyone what I know,
how it feels to be stripped and plucked.

—Deborah Gerrish

Craft Tip #8: Concrete Details: Making the World Material

—David Bottoms

Creative writing teachers are always telling us to be concrete, be concrete, but rarely does anyone ever stop to tell us why. Flannery O'Connor clears this up fairly quickly in an essay called "The Nature and Aim of Fiction":

> The nature of fiction is in large measure determined by the nature of our perceptive apparatus. The beginning of human knowledge is through the senses, and the fiction writer begins where human perception begins.

And so does the poet. Everything we know of the world, we know by virtue of our five senses. We walk around and our senses gather data. We see, we touch, we hear, we smell, we taste. The nerves send this information to the brain and the brain jumbles it all up and comes up with what we call ideas, or abstractions.

One of the biggest problems I encounter in beginning poetry workshops is the desire many inexperienced poets have to be philosophers. They want their poems to be *deep* but often mistake poetry for philosophy. Karl Shapiro, in his essay "What is Not Poetry," says, *If poetry has an opposite, it is philosophy. Poetry is a materialization of experience; philosophy is the abstraction of it.* That merits some thought.

For years now, I've told this little story to illustrate the point. A poet and a philosopher are walking across Woodruff Park, going over to Fairlie-Poplar for some Thai food. When they reach Peachtree Street, they see a yellow flash go by, then hear a gigantic crash under the traffic light. A yellow MG has tried to beat the light and smashed into the side of a furniture truck. It's a mess. Well, the poet and the philosopher rush over and try to help. A crowd gathers, and somebody's on a cell phone calling an ambulance. Gasoline, blood, and glass are everywhere. The philosopher takes it all in and immediately starts to abstract. He ponders for a moment, then mutters, *Accident, Fate, Death.*

The poet, on the other hand, whips out her notebook and writes down everything that happened: the yellow flash on Peachtree Street, the smell of the smoking brakes, the spilled gasoline, the sound of the impact, the blood in the street. She goes back to her apartment and fleshes it out on a legal pad as vividly as she can; then she types it up into a poem called "Smash Up" and sends it to *The New Yorker*. We read it in Barnes & Noble a few months later. We pause for a moment, then think, *Accident, Fate, Death*. The point is this: The poet and the philosopher are both traveling to the same city. The poet is simply taking the scenic route. The poet is trying to make the world material on the page, so that the reader can abstract, so that the reader can take what clues the world offers and decipher meaning from them. The poet wants the reader to participate, to experience the event vividly.

As writers we want to affect our readers in the most immediate way. Years ago, I asked a class to write a poem describing something hot, say an atomic bomb. Half the class was to use only abstract words, the other half only concrete words. The abstract poems came out something like this: Poem 1: *The atomic bomb / is very hot*. Poem 2, somewhat hotter: *The atomic bomb / is very very hot.* Poem 3, hottest of all: *The atomic bomb is extremely very very hot.*

The other half of the class turned in poems that appealed more directly to the senses, as does Philip Levine when he describes the intensity of the fireball from the atomic blast at Hiroshima. This is from his early poem "The Horse":

> They spoke of the horse alive
> without skin, naked, hairless,
> without eyes and ears, searching
> for the stable boy's caress.
> Shoot it, someone said, but they
> let it go on colliding with
>
> tattered walls, butting his long
> skull to pulp, finding no path
> where iron fences corkscrewed in
> the street and bicycles turned
> like question marks.

> Some fled and
> some sat down. The river burned
> all that day and into the
> night, the stones sighed a moment
> and were still, and the shadow
> of a man's hand entered
> a leaf.

Iron fences have been melted into corkscrews, stones have expanded and are sighing as they cool, the shadow of a man's hand has entered a leaf. Now that is undeniably hot. The contrast here is startling. And it points to the fundamental weakness of all abstractions. That is simply that abstractions cannot communicate a sense of degree. A poet may very easily say that something is hot, but if she wants to say *how* hot it is, she must deal with the concrete.

Ask yourself these questions: Do you want to let your reader participate in the world, let your reader share your experience? Then, *Be concrete!* Do you want to touch your reader in the most dynamic way, to affect your reader at the most immediate level? Then, *Be concrete!* Do you want to express the depth, the degree, the intensity to which you feel something? Then, well, you know.

Poem and Prompt

Unfurlings

Unroll every saved piece
and parcel and
dream, every love
letter, recipe, nightmare
you dare not tell
before breakfast (bad
luck), every thrown away
blouse, too tight
denim, the outgrown,
the faded, the lost and
the never to come again
moment, the trees
as they gathered the two
of you into their shadows
then let you go
as you knew they had
to, but here
lie the unfoldings,
coffee-stained,
wine splashed and
wrinkled, the grimy,
the silly, the lists
you forgot to take
with you each day
into the rest of your life,
here your life
itself spread on
the table and you left
to call it whatever

it means, clutter,
kindling, or
cast aside wings
you almost believe
you could let fly.

—Kathryn Stripling Byer

At one time or another, we are all confronted with the task of cleaning out a space—an entire house or apartment, a room, a closet, a drawer. This can be a happy chore or a gut-wrenching one, sometimes both.

The speaker in Byer's poem provides details that let us know her space was inhabited by two people (*the trees / as they gathered the two / of you...*) and for a long time. Notice that the speaker is not one of the two people but addresses them as *you*. Or perhaps she has stepped outside of herself and is speaking to herself. The use of second person point of view creates emotional distance.

The poem is structured as a catalog, a list of what must be cleaned out. The list combines concrete, tangible items such as *every love / letter, recipe* and the *too tight denim* with more abstract items such as every *dream... / nightmare / you dare not tell*. There are love letters, but there are also *shadows* and things that are *grimy*. These details do not tell the story of a life but provide a sense of a life, one lived fully with its joys and sorrows. Contraries! Remember, we love them.

Notice the strategic line breaks, e.g., *every love / letter* and *bad / luck*. Such breaks offer both double meaning and surprise. Notice also the shape of the poem. With its long skinny form, the poem looks like an unfurling or unfolding. There is meaning even in the form. Notice, too, how the poem builds to a lovely metaphor at the end.

Here's your challenge. First, think of a space that needs uncluttering. Or perhaps a space you already cleared out. Or someone else cleared out. Compile a list of the material items. Then add some less tangible items, some conceptual items. Strive for a mixture of light and shadow.

Using second person point of view, write your first draft drawing from the material in your list.

Rearrange the order of the lines. Be sure that the items are mixed, not all the good, then all the bad, though surely one may predominate. End with a metaphor. Don't settle for the first one that comes to you. Try a variety. Keep going until the just right one emerges.

For your title you might strive for the metaphorical kind that Byer has achieved. Or you might create a title something like "Cleaning Out the Jewelry Box," which locates the poem, or "After the Divorce" which provides background information and sets the tone for the poem.

Sample Poems

Pieces

I set aside pieces of furniture, clothing, more books than my own shelves can hold—the ones she loved most and titled spines I remember from childhood, can see even now with my eyes closed. I place DuMaurier's *Frenchman's Creek* into a carton marked "keep" and wrap her jewelry box in tissue paper to take with me (as if any one of those small, bright rings on my own finger might bring her hands back into being).

The sky goes dark, loosely draped with white night-clouds. Stars gather in windows scored with memories of light that burned out long before any of us was here. Shadows flicker on the edge of sight—a sigh, a laugh hauntingly far away. I pack dresses and shoes, take down the last of the hangers and close the door to her bedroom. There's no way back to what was, only these rooms filled with new silence, a house to be emptied and sold.

It's true that we lose their voices first (inflection, tone), and I haven't learned how to reconcile this listening with the voice I can no longer hear. There's no formula for letting go of the old, gone world or this house where every ordinary thing has become more than it is.

—Adele Kenny
published in *Paterson Literary Review*

On Hoarding

Every morning I walk by the hoarders' house,
a perpetually deferred garage sale
in progress—
or should I say regress—
because they've outgrown the house
of their lives,

colonized the front yard
with old Atari games, seedy bird cages,
Chutes and Ladders,
video cassettes whose tapes must stretch for miles,
their cartridges unwinding
a narrative of loss.

Maybe their marriage too is unwinding,
their children moved on.
Yet it's brave,
the way, having filled every room in the house,
they've put their former dailiness
on show,

stacked it up like home-grown produce
at a county fair,
or packed it in open-topped boxes
covered with tarps
so winter rain won't defile these sad,
rejected Lares.

I almost envy their hoarding, its refusal
to part with the past.
I've thrown so much away, things that held me,
cushioned chairs and dream-stained
sheets,
a mirror's fickle light.

—Jeanne Wagner
published in *Connotation Press*

Craft Tip #9: Write to the Barrette

—Jill Alexander Essbaum

Oh, Michael Stipe. Yes, yes. It's true. Everybody hurts. Sometimes.

But what about that day in mid-October 1986 when Tabitha Q. Weatherbee stayed after school to ask her algebra teacher, Lester Higginbotham, to explain polynomials and he locked the door behind her and grabbed her right breast so hard that she wore a saffron yellow bruise for a week?

And dear Mister Darin. You can do better than that nebulous anywhere you've sung out as that *somewhere* that lies *beyond the sea. The* sea? Which one? No one's saying you have to name it outright. But criminy. Give us *something.* The west waters where the grey birds fight over fish? The choppy waters no one but pirates ever bothered to chart? Those unnavigable blacks, deep as death that float at the bottom of the planet?

Of course, I'm exaggerating to make a point: Our tendency as poets is to write *big.* By that I mean we have big ideas and big hearts and we, like those Christmastide singers of years ago, want to teach the world to sing—the whole freaking world!—to sing along with us, our song. Our song might be sad, our song might be political or poignant or passionate or all or none of the above, but because we're poets, there's a good chance that when we come to the page it's because we care deeply about the art

And we want you—and you, and you, and you, and every you everywhere and anywhere—to care about it, too. And to find meaning in it. And to relate to it. And to be moved. That's just natural.

In the case of so many beginning poets, the urge is to forgo the specific in favor of the general. Because surely what's general is more inclusive, yes? Because to pin down a place, a person, an instance, an image is to lock out a hundred other experiences, right?

No. There's the paradox. The rub-a-dub-dub. The whiz-bang of it all.

Consider the following exceptionally tragic scenario: a mother burying an infant. There's little sadder than that. Few things scrape a bone so empty.

First go: *She watched the funeral director close the coffin. Her infant daughter was inside. She would never see her again. It was the saddest she had ever felt. Would ever feel.*

Admittedly, it's an intentionally rough cut set of sentences, open-ended on purpose. Even so, I'll admit it again: I recognize my own tendencies here. The bigness of the sad! The saddest-ness! The never-dom! And while I've avoided legitimate abstractions, there's nothing so specific that I can walk away from this short paragraph with enough confidence to announce that no one but Jill Alexander Essbaum could have composed this collection of sentences.

Now try this: *Momma dressed the baby in the pale peach gown she'd planned for her to wear at her christening. It hadn't been ironed yet. She'd run out of time. They'd snapped a matching barrette onto that one downy forelock of hair. But the hair was so fine and the teeth of the barrette barely caught it. After they closed the coffin, and all through the service, and into the next week, and the next, Momma couldn't stop fretting over that barrette. Whether it stayed put. Whether it fell off. Whether she buried her daughter with pretty hair or not.*

Which one's sadder?

If I were working this into a poem, of course, I'd prune it, hone it, spitshine it. But the exercise is a good one in any case.

The thing is, you really do want to walk away from one of your poems being able to honestly announce, *This is all and only mine.* Remember: the specific is the universal. The more you smallify your thoughts, the more you bigify them. Go straight to the barrette. Everything else will work itself out.

I promise.

Poem and Prompt

Requiem

> *Sing the mass—*
> *light upon me washing words*
> *now that I am gone.*

The sky was a hot, blue sheet the summer breeze fanned
out and over the town. I could have lived forever
under that sky. Forgetting where I was,
I looked left, not right, crossed into a street
and stepped in front of the bus that ended me.

Will you believe me when I tell you it was beautiful—
my left leg turned to uselessness and my right shoe flung
some distance down the road? Will you believe me
when I tell you I had never been so in love
with anyone as I was, then, with everyone I saw?

The way an age-worn man held his wife's shaking arm,
supporting the weight that seemed to sing from the heart
she clutched. Knowing her eyes embraced the pile
that was me, he guided her sacked body through the crowd.
And the way one woman began a fast the moment she looked

under the wheel. I saw her swear off decadence.
I saw her start to pray. You see, I was so beautiful
the woman sent to clean the street used words
like police tape to keep back a young boy
seconds before he rounded the grisly bumper.

The woman who cordoned the area feared my memory
would fly him through the world on pinions of passion
much as, later, the sight of my awful beauty pulled her down
to tears when she pooled my blood with water
and swiftly, swiftly washed my stains away.

                    —Camille Dungy

A *requiem* is a poem in honor of the dead. Dungy begins hers with an epigraph. This serves as a lens through which we read the poem. While an epigraph is usually drawn from another work by someone else, here the epigraph is by Dungy. It immediately brings to mind a requiem mass and gets us ready for the poem.

Dungy offers a compelling variation of tradition as the speaker recounts the moment of her own death. Our dead speaker tells us that she was distracted by the beauty of the sky and carelessly stepped in front of a bus. This information is followed by two questions and then the reactions of several people who witnessed the death. Stanzas 3, 4, and 5 list and detail those reactions.

The tone throughout the poem is intriguing. Although getting hit by a bus hardly strikes us as a lovely way to go, the speaker expresses amazement at the beauty of her death. Her direct address to the auditor/reader establishes a tone of intimacy. It also pulls us into the scene and makes us witnesses.

The formal structure of the poem—five 5-line stanzas—seems appropriate to the occasion of a requiem and subtly adds to the tone, giving the poem a feeling of reverence.

Notice the strategic use of repetition in the poem, e.g., there is anaphora in stanza 2 as the two questions begin with *Will you believe me when I tell you...?* In stanza 4 *I saw* begins two sentences. Then the repetition of *swiftly* in the poem's last line emphasizes the action and adds a touch of irony as it slows down the line.

Finally, notice the perfect iambic pentameter line that closes the poem. This makes for a powerful ending.

For your own requiem poem, first imagine the manner of your or your speaker's death. With that in mind, describe the scene, including ample details. Just let the details flow out of you.

Speak directly to the auditor/reader, addressing him or her as *you* or perhaps by name.

Use some repetition in your poem.

Can you find or create an appropriate epigraph? This isn't essential, but give it a try.

In subsequent drafts, as you feel that you are nearing your final draft, give your poem a formal structure. Don't do this too early in the drafting as doing so tends to shut down thinking; instead of generating new material, you might concentrate on making the material fit your chosen format.

Try to get your last line in iambic pentameter.

Alternative topic: the moment of your birth or the moment of your conception.

Sample Poems

Things Were Looking Up

I was sitting at the kitchen table, in your seat
where I always sat after you died, winter light
metallic, as if the snow were chrome, watching
the shadows lengthen and thin to extinction.

For a long time, I'd eaten in the den, with the TV,
but then I'd returned to my own company
and on the night I died I was very happy.
It had been a good day.

So it was a good day to die. It worked like this:
first there was panic, the rib I'd cracked a week before
preventing me from mustering a cough
sufficient to dislodge the crust in my throat—

whole body struggling as if re-computing,
scrambling for an alternate route, and then
it knew, and it stopped fighting.
Everything opened—my pores, my eyes,

wide and dilated, my tongue tingling.
I shivered, once, felt a moment of dizziness,
and fell unconscious. Choked to death—
though I was still alive for a while

even after I no longer breathed, fed
by oxygen stored in my blood, sap flowing
back to my trunk from all my branches,
answering the weakened cricket summons of my heart.

It was a good day to die. The snow was melting,
spring assuredly on its way, and dinner was delicious.
I'd indulged earlier in a bubble bath and whispered
a few good words onto a page—which always

made me happy. My rib no longer ached as badly
as it had, and the walkway where I had fallen
was no longer icy. Things were looking up.
And you, my love, you'd gone so long before.

—Lisken Van Pelt Dus

The Moment I Realized Looks Were Nothing At All

What we imagine is of no worth
is the very crown and scepter
of divine Grace.
        —Joe Weil

It surprised me last year when a friend called me pretty.
I had so wanted to be, all my life. I hadn't liked the clothes
Mom put me in, navy blue, hated the pixie haircut instead
of my friend's long curls, bemoaned braces and thrift stores.

Despised the football player I loved in seventh grade,
who turned around, unasked, and said "I don't like you."
And "You're so flat your children will starve to death
if you nurse them, but at least you won't get breast cancer."

And how something tragic happened to his child, and I hated
how I instantly thought *karma*. Hated having said stupid things,
said a fat classmate "had a beautiful soul." If I couldn't be foxy,
I decided instead to cultivate the hot confidence of wit.

And then, Simone Weil, lightning bolt:
"A beautiful woman looking at her image
may very well believe the image is herself.
An ugly woman knows it is not."

Beauty, you didn't really matter, did you?
Who gave me wrong instructions from the start?
The hours (years if you add them up) wasted watching weight,
counting blemishes, fretting over fashion, disregarding accidents

of genetics, as if I'd earned this straight nose somehow.
What books could I have read, what friendships made,
and insights shared, if those thoughts had, as in men,
seldom surfaced? What gifts could I have given?

        —Tina Kelley

The Poet on the Poem: Susan Laughter Meyers

Coastland

When the wind gets up and the water rises,
those who live on higher ground, at a distance
from the pinched smell of pluff mud,
from spartina marshes and swamps of cypress knees,
upland from the tannin-black tributaries
where through the bottoms, among the wet-footed
spider lilies, one barred owl
calls another, one to the other till there's little left to say,
upland from the cottonmouth and the brown water snake
coiled and rooted by the tupelo
and the alligators logging across the slough,
upland from the deer hound pens full of yelps—
full of naps and pacing, full of cedar-thicket dreaming—
and the dirt yard's milling of gray cats
and striped kittens yawning by the palmettos,
upland from the sea sky sea—the horizon
a fine line polished away—
from the shrimp boats shrinking smaller and smaller
on their way to their serious work of gathering,
from the smooth, quick balancing act
of the sun—heavy and orange—riding the waves,
upland from salt myrtle and the season's second growth
of trumpet honeysuckle, those who live at a distance
from the band of quick, dark clouds blooming at sea,
upland from the bang and whirl, clatter
and shake of the wind when it's up,
those who live on higher ground ask
of those who live by the flats and shoals,
the shallows and bogs, Why, and again, Why, O why.

DL: The diction in your poem is wonderful, e.g., *pluff mud, spartina marshes, wet-footed spider lilies, salt myrtle, trumpet honeysuckle*. How did you acquire all these succulent words? Did they appear in your first draft or did you add them to the poem during revision?

SLM: From the poem's inception I knew that I would be knee-deep in language and sound. There were twenty-six drafts—and from the start the poem included image after image from the natural world; but of the ones you pointed out, only the trumpet honeysuckle was in the first draft. By draft three, though, the pluff mud and spartina marshes were there, as well as the spider lilies—though they weren't wet-footed yet. So it was an early, but gradual, process—the accretion of language and imagery—and it's a boon to us poets that the names for native flora and fauna are rich in sound.

DL: I very much admire the way you've succeeded in animating the setting. Tell us how you created the sense of motion and energy that pervades the poem.

SLM: I wrote the poem not long after the active hurricane season of 2005, the year of Hurricanes Katrina and Rita among others. So the sheer energy of the storms was still with me. Despite the danger from hurricanes, the love for the lowlands and the wild beauty there persisted in my mind. More than once I've been in the situation of whether or not to evacuate—and if so, when—and it's hard to leave, despite the danger. I wanted to show the attachment to the land, to a way of life, to the wild and even the less-than-beautiful aspects of the coastal plains.

Most of the images that came to mind as I was writing have their own motion of some kind—the snakes and alligators, the owls, the shrimp boats at work—that energy plus the force of the wind in the poem, always the wind—well, all of these, together with the fear, attachment, and uncertainty stirred up by the storm at hand, contributed to my own sense of agitation and unrest. And I hope that the swirling energy was conveyed.

DL: One of the feats of this poem is its syntax. How difficult was it to get one long sentence to sustain the entire poem? Tell us, also, about the function of the dashes.

SLM: I love what syntax can do in a poem, its ability to indicate not just sequence but also hierarchy and relationships, its role in manipulating the rhythm and pacing. Syntax is truly like a conductor leading an orchestra. Because "Coastland" consists of a sustained list, it felt natural for it to be one long, convoluted sentence. I wanted the movement of the poem to be somewhat like a spring that uncoils, a movement that seemed fitting for a poem about wind.

As you can tell, I'm fond of dashes. I often use them to interrupt myself or to set off an explanatory phrase, sometimes for the extra-long pause that I'm aiming for. Other times I use them because I've already used commas, and further commas to set off the phrase or clause would simply be confusing.

DL: Your use of anaphora is hypnotic and all the more impressive because it occurs within one long sentence. The repetition of *upland from* and *from the* scattered throughout the poem adds speed and intensity. How did you decide how much was enough and not too much?

SLM: I did play around with that as I revised, but actually the frequency of those repetitions settled in sooner than I expected, probably because I kept reading the poem aloud. That's the only way I can make those sorts of decisions, to hear the rhythms and patterns sounded out in different ways. While I'm reading my poems aloud, I hold my hand up close in front of my mouth so that the sound bounces back to my ears. Then, and only then, can I begin to tell what is and isn't working.

DL: Although there's no end rhyme, you make the poem sing with other sound devices—alliteration, assonance, consonance, and monosyllabic words. Tell us about the craft decisions that resulted in the poem's music.

SLM: I try to follow sound whenever I can. Thus, when I make diction choices, they're often based on sound. The more I do this, the more it becomes natural to me. As a result, my ear is becoming more attuned to sound patterns. Reading the poem aloud comes into play, too. One example from the poem is those spider lilies mentioned earlier. In an early draft the image focused on *the spider lilies' white thin stars*, referring to the narrow-leaved white flowers of native spider lilies that grow in swamps and along the edges of rivers. I liked the description of the flowers fine, but the image didn't seem to do anything for the sound and rhythm of the poem. Eventually the wording became *the wet-footed / spider lilies,* which meant a loss of the flowers as stars but a gain of the rhythm and sound repetition in *wet-footed.* That's the kind of change I'll make for the sake of a poem's music.

My reading directly affects my craft decisions, too. I seek out poems by other poets that are musical, hoping to learn from them. There are so many decisions to make! Thank goodness, many of them are ones we're not even conscious of when we make them. Some of those good, unnoticed decisions derive from the bones of our writing practice—and old failed poems.

Bonus Prompt: Scavenger Poem

Look out the nearest window and quickly jot down the names of five concrete objects that you see outside.

Then write a quick description of each object.

Next write one metaphor or simile for each object.

Now draft a new poem in which you use all five descriptions and metaphors but not the names of the objects.

Later, put the names of the objects back in, but use a dictionary and the internet to find the best words. Don't be satisfied with *shrub* or *tree*.

This may be difficult, but that's a good thing. This will challenge your descriptive powers.

IV. Syntax, Line, Spacing

Poetry is not only dream and vision; it is the skeleton architecture of our lives.

—Audre Lorde

Craft Tip #10: Syntax in Poetry

—Priscilla Orr

Someone once asked me if I love making poems because I love words. What I couldn't articulate then was that I feel the poem in the form of music—inner rhythms—before I ever get to the page. Syntax, of course, is a huge part of that experience.

Great poems marry image and sound with language; syntax is the medium for synthesizing these elements. It will help us, as poets, to know that the part of the brain that learns language and word order is the same part of the brain that processes music. By employing syntactical strategies, we can make our poems both more musical and more effective. I'd like to talk about several of these strategies: anaphora, conditional clauses, fractured syntax, and rhythmic counterpoint.

1. Anaphora
Anaphora is the repetition of a phrase at the beginning of lines or sentences. In Jane Kenyon's poem, "Let Evening Come," the imperative phrase *Let the light*...is repeated throughout the poem though the word *light* is substituted by other words. This repetition is combined with the repetition of the phrase *Let evening come*. Both elements work to unify the poem and create its music:

> Let the light of late afternoon
> shine through chinks in the barn, moving
> up the bales as the sun moves down.
>
> Let the cricket take up chafing
> as a woman takes up her needles
> and her yarn. Let evening come.

Because Kenyon sets up a declarative syntactical structure that continues throughout the poem, we come to expect it as a refrain from a song or hymn. She varies the structure only in the second to the last stanza, but by then the rhythmic pattern has been established and internalized by the reader. If we read the poem aloud, we feel the musical phrasing even before we stop to understand the meaning of the stanzas.

2. Conditional Clauses
Such clauses are also known as *if clauses*. They can begin a poem or be injected elsewhere in the poem. Take a look at how Stanley Kunitz begins his poem, "King of the River":

> If the water were clear enough,
> if the water were still,
> but the water is not clear,
> the water is not still,
> you would see yourself,
> slipped out of your skin

Kunitz not only sets up the conditional phrase beginning with *If*, but also undermines the condition by contradicting it with *but* and *not*. He then picks up where the conditional phrase left off. This syntactical structure is reiterated in four of the poem's five stanzas. The poem thus takes on a kind of mythic quality, and we feel we are in sacred territory.

The poet keeps us waiting for the lines or words that will complete the sentence. By doing so, he keeps us suspended in the poem. This technique allows the sentence to go on and on at length, gathering momentum as it does. Other clauses that can work similarly may begin with such words as *although*, *when*, and *because*.

3. Fractured Syntax
With this strategy the poet changes the order of the sentence in unexpected ways. The fractured syntax can add emphasis to meaning. In Gregory Orr's poem, "A Moment," syntax is crucial in allowing the speaker to create the distance needed to talk about a very dramatic subject—how he accidentally killed his own brother:

> The field where my brother died—
> I've walked there since.

Notice how Orr delays the direct action of the sentence by fracturing the syntax. Instead of saying, *I've walked the field where my brother died*, he puts us in the field, immediately making his brother's death the true subject of the sentence. Later, he also uses a declarative sentence with a colon:

> I still can see: a father
> and his sons bent above
> a deer they'd shot,
> then screams and shouts.

The colon fractures the smooth flow of the sentence and forces us to pause and see what the speaker sees—that he has just accidentally shot his brother. The deftness of the syntax keeps the poem from being sentimental.

4. Rhythmic Counterpoint
Using this technique, the poet resists the rhythm of the speaking voice. Similar to fracturing the syntax, breaking the rhythm of the speaker's voice can add an emotional resonance that mimes the content of the poem. Take Yusef Koumanyakaa's famous poem, "Facing It," in which the speaker, a Viet Nam vet, stands in front of the memorial in Washington, D.C.:

> The sky. A plane in the sky.
> A white vet's image floats
> closer to me, then his pale eyes
> look through mine. I'm a window.
> He's lost his right arm
> inside the stone. In the black mirror
> a woman's trying to erase names:

The poet moves from fragments to a complete sentence, from objective passive description to the personal *I* as the subject of the sentence, *I'm a window*. He goes back and forth from what he sees to what he is. Then he shifts his gaze to a woman. Notice that the last sentence switches syntax and begins with a prepositional phrase.

We think of the emotional power of a poem as coming from its imagery and music. However, the syntax of Koumanyakaa's lines mimics the speaker's disorientation and helps the images do their work more effectively. All of these elements contribute to the emotional power of the poem.

Paying attention to syntax shakes us out of our ingrained sense of rhythm and sentence structure. We need to be able to use syntax in different ways. Doing so will yield surprises, create music, intensify feeling, and deepen meaning in our work.

Poem and Prompt

Every Great Novel Ends in Sleep

Since we cannot meet in this world,
we agree to meet in *Anna Karenina*, page 18
in the Garnett translation. While Vronsky
arrives in Krasnoe and hands the footman his hat,
while Tolstoy fusses over plausible details—
moldy arras? leaky samovar? snuffling stallion?
deafening crickets?—we slip into the boathouse
to undo pearl buttons with a shaky hand. Soon
startled swifts volley—will they hurt themselves
against the low rafters?—and a bittern cries.
Or are there loons in Russia? Are there butterflies
with eyes on their wings, this deep in the past?
All we can do is lie still and tremble.
We listen to the pulse like children
intent on a conch. We sense a licked finger
touching the page at the upper-right corner,
twilight buckles between us, and we turn,
since we cannot meet in this world.

—D. Nurkse

The speaker in this poem imagines an assignation with a real woman in an unreal world, the world of a book. Because the woman is one who arouses desire, the speaker chooses an appropriately romantic novel, page 18 to be exact. We do not know the identity of the lover or why the speaker cannot meet her in this world. By withholding this information, Nurkse adds mystery and danger. As the speaker and his lover meet clandestinely in the boathouse, he imagines the writer at work and speculates about the details Tolstoy might be laboring over.

He then imagines the sexiness of a *licked finger* turning to page 19. The couple goes deeper into the book until finally, as the title foretells, they sleep.

Notice that the speaker uses the first person plural point of view. This increases the feeling of intimacy. We have a collective of just two.

The poem's syntax is skillfully handled. The first sentence begins with a dependent clause. The second begins with two dependent clauses, followed by the interruption of four short questions set off by dashes, followed by an independent clause. The third sentence is a compound one interrupted in the middle by another question. Then we have two interrogative sentences, followed by three declarative sentences, the last one a compound sentence that ends with the very clause that began the poem, completing a lovely circle and providing a feeling of containment.

For your own poem, choose a novel or perhaps a movie into which you (or your speaker) will escape with someone you'd like to spend time with but cannot in this world. This might or might not be someone you know. Or perhaps you'd prefer to escape by yourself. If your speaker escapes with another person, use first person plural point of view.

Zero in on a particular scene of the novel or movie. Paint the scene with concrete details from your chosen work.

Imitate some of the syntactical structures Nurkse uses.

Include some questions and some dashes.

Try beginning and ending your poem with the same line.

Think carefully about your title. See if you can create one that foreshadows the end of the poem.

Sample Poems

Since We No Longer Can Meet

—in this world that is, let's meet in Judy Blume's new novel. In December, Nia's on Broad Street, the lingerie shop where Miri chooses her mother's birthday gift, where I'll choose one for you. Because you are gone, have been gone for thirty years, because you couldn't be there—it's a surprise—you could hide your ghostly presence in the dressing room behind velvet curtains, your thoughts could control me as they did, still do. Don't remind me that your birthday heralds summer, we're in a book—fiction, remember? It's the frigid winter of a New Jersey town's terror, planes plunge from the sky—dancers' feet stilled, new loves hushed by flames, homes in ashes. Oh how planes terrified you. You didn't fear lingerie though, your long brassiere hooked into the eyes of your corset, its bones grooving flesh ladders along your hips. While you hide, you'll instruct, *no, don't buy that bra, not that corset, see the navy half-slip, double slits? Vanity Fair, only $3.99, it looks like smoke, a wisp. Tell Nia you want it.* I'll argue with you, *Ma, it's only a book, we're in a novel, the slip isn't real, you'd never wear anything like that, you hated the Pucci copy I bought you at Saks in 1967, remember? You asked where the top of that slip was.* Let's meet again, Ma, let's meet again, let's meet in Judy Blume's new novel at Nia's—or anywhere.

—Gail Fishman Gerwin
published in *Ithaca Lit*

Reading Alcott, 1962

Of course I knew she'd written the whole thing
almost a hundred years ago, when people were
lots more used to that kind of dismal stuff.
But by chapter 36 it was pretty clear to me
that Beth was going to die (and really soon).
I couldn't stand it. *Louisa May!* I cried out
from the depths of my soul, *How could you
do this? How could you kill her?*

And then I'd think about my own sister Pam
with her orange bangs and denim pedal-pushers
stretched out in a four-poster bed under a faded quilt.
She'd be way too weak for needlework by now,
so I'd bring her chamomile tea in a china cup
and bend over her counterpane in my long, dark
dress (what's a counterpane, anyway?) crooning
something like, *The New Year's Eve we did the town,
the day we tore the goalposts down,* and Pam
would shoot me a trembly smile and slurp some tea.

Read me a story, she would beg, *to guide me
to the promised land.* So I'd take my grimy copy
of *Tropic of Cancer* out of my pocket and read to her
from the best parts. She'd ask me to read some of them
again and again. Then she'd close her eyes
and we would speak quietly of the cute new boy
who'd moved into the house next door. His name
would be Laurie. And then she'd make me promise
that the minute she died I had to go over there
and ask him if he wanted to go to the funeral with me
and take in a movie afterwards. Or a play, or
whatever they had in those days. And I would nod
bravely and say yes, of course I would. Of course.

—Marilyn L. Taylor

Craft Tip #11: This Is Just To Say: On Line Breaks

—Timothy Liu

Here's a method I use to take a closer look at line breaks. Choose a short poem that you admire, say "The Red Wheelbarrow" by William Carlos Williams, and take out all the line breaks, reprinting the poem on the page as prose like this:

> so much depends upon a red wheel barrow glazed with rain water beside the white chickens

Notice that this particular poem does not use any punctuation or caps. Good! Let several hours or days go by. Then return to the prose version of the poem. Now, to the best of your recollection, write out the poem by hand with what you believe are the original line and stanza breaks. Then check your work against the original. Does your poem look like the following:

> so much depends
> upon
>
> a red wheel
> barrow
>
> glazed with rain
> water
>
> beside the white
> chickens

What choices did Williams make about the couplets? How would you describe their appearance? Three words followed by one word. Repeated four times. A sixteen word poem.

Now review the parts of speech for each terminal word:

> depends: verb
> upon: preposition
> wheel: adjective

barrow: noun
rain: adjective
water: noun
white: adjective
chickens: plural noun

Notice the dance among different parts of speech, the energy that accrues. Williams splits those compound nouns across the line break into adjective/noun pairs. By using enjambment in this manner, the poet brings a series of small surprises into the poem.

Williams said a poem is *a little machine made out of words*. By taking his contraptions apart, then putting them back together, all the while noticing what kinds of patterns he employs for his lines and stanzas (as well as his parts of speech and use of punctuation), we are then able to bring that kind of attention to our own poems.

Here's a longer poem by Williams, again with the line and stanza breaks stripped out:

> This is just to say I have eaten the plums that were in the icebox and which you were probably saving for breakfast Forgive me they were delicious so sweet and so cold

What do you think the original poem looked like? Get out a sheet of paper and give it a try! A few hints: the title of the poem is included in the passage. Also, the poem is staged as three quatrains.

Once you've given it your best shot, find the original. What patterns do the lines and stanzas make? What parts of speech serve as anchor words for each line? What do you notice about the poet's use of caps or lack of punctuation?

Now take a poem of your own that you are stuck on, a poem that doesn't look or feel right on the page in terms of its line and stanza breaks. Strip out all those breaks and leave what remains as a prose block. Then with curiosity and gusto, employ fresh strategies and a new structure to recast your prose block into something more exciting.

Poem and Prompt

Vex Me

Vex me, O Night, your stars stuttering like a stuck jukebox,
put a spell on me, my bones atremble at your tabernacle

of rhythm and blues. Call out your archers, chain me
to a wall, let the stone fortress of my body fall

like a rabid fox before an army of dogs. Rebuke me,
rip out my larynx like a lazy snake and feed it to the voiceless

throng. For I am midnight's girl, scouring unlit streets
like Persephone stalking her swarthy lord. Anoint me

with oil, make me greasy as a fast-food fry. Deliver me
like a pizza to the snapping crack-house hours between

one and four. Build me an ark, fill it with prairie moths,
split-winged fritillaries, blue-bottle flies. Stitch

me a gown of taffeta and quinine, starlight and nightsoil,
and when the clock tocks two, I'll be the belle of the malaria ball.

—Barbara Hamby

Hamby's poem of supplication is immediately distinguished by
its strong voice, a quality achieved by several methods. The
speaker's direct address to the Night is pleading but also
insistent. The imperative sentences with their strong verbs give
additional power to the voice: *Vex me, Call out, Rebuke me,
Anoint me, Deliver me, Build me, Stitch me.* The parallel
structure and repetition in that list of imperatives reinforce the
insistence and add music. The voice is further enhanced by the series

of verbs that Hamby strings together within sentences: *Call out... chain me...let*; *Rebuke me, rip out...feed it*; *Anoint me...make me greasy.*

Another engaging quality of this poem is its inventive metaphors: *the stone fortress of my body, I am midnight's girl,* and *I'll be the belle of the malaria ball.* The metaphors are joined by a string of zany similes: *like a rabid fox, like a lazy snake, greasy as a fast-food fry,* and *like a pizza.*

The irony of the supplicant begging and demanding to be abased and the freshness and surprise of the figures add a delightful humor to the poem, a quality not easily accomplished.

The poet also employs several devices of sound. Notice, for example, the assonance of *build, fill, fritillaries, unlit, split,* and *stitch.* Notice the consonance of *vex, jukebox,* and *larynx.* Finally, notice the rhymes and near rhymes scattered throughout the poem: *oil, soil, call, wall, fall, belle, ball.*

Consider, too, the form of the poem. Sonnet-like with its 14 lines, it has a shift right in the middle at line 7. Here the sentence structure changes and a mythological allusion enters the poem. Hamby organizes the poem into 2-line stanzas and uses enjambment at the end of every line and from stanza to stanza. This creates an energetic pace and yields one surprise after the other as we move from line ending to line beginning.

Now let's write a poem of supplication. First decide what your speaker will speak to. Maybe the Sun, Shade, Wind, Grass, Dirt. It should be something not human, but you will address it as if it were human.

Brainstorm a list of self-abasing demands to make of your subject.

Begin your draft using direct address. As you incorporate your list of demands, use imperative sentences and strong verbs.

Work in some inventive metaphors and similes. Be fanciful, not sensible. Be abundant.

As you get several drafts along, work on the sound devices. Pick a word used early in the poem and create a list of rhymes and near rhymes. Scatter the words from your list throughout the rest of the poem.

As you revise, work on the form of your poem. You might choose to use Hamby's structure, but consider other options as well. Do be sure, though, to use some enjambment and to break your sentence pattern at least once in the poem.

Sample Poems

Synthesis

Oh Rock in my Path, how considerate of you to descend
early in the morning to avoid squashing my flesh-bag

beneath your magnificence. Oh pristine mineral-boulder
from above, forgive me my crane-dance of frustration

at the thought of detouring back down the winding trail.
It's the idea that I might fail that vexed me, hexed me

into the prevailing arm flailing you may have observed.
Sparkle at me, you quartz wonder, in shades of milk

and jasper. I'll bow before your stern rebuke like wheat
nods to the west wind. Forgive me the urge to reach up

and pluck out your amethyst eye. It is more beautiful
than silk. Lust in my lilac heart matches the translucent

tetrahedraness displayed this day. Deliver me, jewel, from
the need to crack you with a hammer, to pry loose crystal

shards with torn fingernails that leave traces of buttery blood
on your rotund facade. I keen before your swirled sedimentary

stateliness. Flatten me. I beg you. I will hug your craggy shape
until night pries my chilled fingers free, and sends me running

down the path, where I trip, fall, and become something
primal, your kin, your spiritual child, an oft-rolled stone.

—Constance Brewer

Imprison Me

Imprison me, oh Sleep. Lock me up and discard the key.
Enchant me with your spells and soporific potions.

Let me sail down the river of forgetfulness
into the silky, silent depths of drowsy darkness.

Enshroud me in the deep folds of eternal night. Let me wear you
as a cloak of protection against my own unending thoughts.

Deliver me, oh Hypnos, ruler of sleep, from the relentless terror
that plagues my wakeful hours. Place me under a mindless trance

and douse me with nothingness. Grant me no thoughts,
no consternation, no analysis—permit my brain to breathe without regret.

Soothe my distressed thinking and expunge the memories
that continue to creep like a persistent vine into my wakeful state.

Absorb the pain of remembrance. Dissuade the thoughts that wait
to pounce on me at light of day. Seize me now and grant me peace.

—Kim Klugh

Craft Tip #12: Blurring the Lines

—Alice B. Fogel

There are important things at stake in a poem's verbal and spatial line breaks. What would happen to the poem—to us!—if we detached ourselves from that safe left margin, that comfortable comma and colon codependence, that cozy breath-based phrasing? What if, being acutely aware of the impact of interactions between lines and their surroundings, we read the silences, distances, and rests of the not-word parts of the poem? These elements of lines' effects are neither merely visual nor merely verbal, and they have an enormous influence on the recursive or circular nature of how we take in pacing, rhythm, suspense, and meaning as we read.

Thinking this way opens up new potential not only for line *placement*, in which the page may be used as a foil for the gathering of information as we read, but also for line *breaks* that syncopate sense. In poetry, the line is one of the most interesting units, with its own rhythms and its intriguing extension towards the unknown at its spatial end. Lines and their breaks delay meaning even as they create it—and this offers readers a desirable tension, a building up of strata, a conversation with content, along with participation in the making of meaning in time.

While still aligned to the left margin, the following is an example of what I mean by syncopation, in which overlapping tiers of meaning unfold as we make our way down the page. This is a section of George Oppen's poem "All This Strangeness":

> desire at the heart of the living
>
> world the poem
>
> spells itself out . . . to say
>
> all you know all
> you are all
> that has happened the world's

While taken out of the full context of the poem, the first line above might still be a complete thought—there is some kind of *desire at the heart of the living*—but when we get to the next line, across the gap of a stanza break, a new completion occurs, so that now we have to change our first thought to desire being *at the heart of the living world*. As we linger in the second line, simultaneously, despite being a sentence fragment, *world the poem* presents its own wholeness. Each time we move onward, a spiraling revision of sense happens: Now, splitting the two nouns from each other in that same line, and going on, *the poem / spells itself out*. Seen likewise on their own, the lines *all you know all* and *you are all* intensify this effect, and as we continue forward, there are multiple readings (or realities) possible: *all you know, all you are* and *you are all that has happened* and *all you know, all you are, all that has happened* [is] *the world's* and *you are...the world's (you belong to the world),* and so on. This suspension of finality excites both mind and body, creates complexity, and confronts us with the limits of our inclinations toward reduction.

Here is an excerpt from "Cornered," one of my own poems:

               this   corner   turning   turned

confounds us enough to sputter

      something about sign and signified   a device at once

   fabricated and otherworldly   the colors

                    of thunder and dusk and fall

      all over ourselves   out of our senses

                          to exist

                    it's enough

         to be in full bodied and silken flight

   turned turning

                 us without referent

     to illusion

"Cornered" was written as a response to a hanging sculpture by the artist and musician Justin Lytle. In an attempt to illustrate the unmoored thrill the artwork always gives me as I stand before it, the poem has a few moments of shifting sense based on line endings, uses no punctuation other than white space, and is not tethered to either margin.

If you have any poems that seem listless or just stuck, try creatively sculpting them to change their impact, either by changing where your lines break, removing punctuation, strategically arranging subordinate clauses, choosing words that afford overlapping meaning, or letting go of the left margin.

Take a look at some poets who challenge our relationship with language and the page. In *Atlas Hour,* Carol Ann Davis sets up her poems along the left margin and then spreads them out as they reach toward the right, so that they look like they are breaking loose from their moorings. Dan Beachy-Quick, in his book *This Nest, Swift Passerine,* alternately moves his poems from left alignment to right to center, making a reader feel a sense of shifting realities. In *The Vital System,* CM Burroughs creates lines that break, turn, and rupture, refusing to let a reader get comfortable and making her poems' fearless concrete imagery even more powerful. Such poets gain traction and emotion from layout on the page.

Poets like these, with their innovative use of lines, breaks, and space, draw our attention back to words' vast possibilities, confronting us with how we collude with unconscious or unacknowledged intentions. They remind us to beware—to be wary, be aware—of language's potentially violent manipulation, achieved through its common invisibility. How these choices upset the status quo and its expectations has the effect of deliberately forcing us to question perception—always one of poetry's top priorities. Whether seen as a political tool or an artistic one (or both), applying new uses of lines and spaces in the crafting of our poems allows us to experience life through words while also experiencing the life of words.

Poem and Prompt

We Call Them Beautiful

We have decided to love trees. The living ones
    are corralled along the sidewalks in cities.
  The dying ones, once glorious,
      collapsed into dust from not being seen.
  Those in forests
    wave their hair and hands whenever the wind blows.

When he runs the track, they are behind him and all around the park.

Against the grey sky, they are like nerves pulled from the body,
    waving, sucking air, sucking dirt.

He starts clean but comes around
    the seventh time sweating, soaking his shirt through,
      giving me a little wave for my whistle.

A sliver of Einstein's brain blown up under the microscope shows
    all the branches
        of where his thoughts went. Still waving.

Around the track the trees wave through the grey afternoon sky,
    like mute women trying to alert me to an emergency.

    —KC Trommer

The first thing that pulls me to this poem is its form, the way it's arranged on the page—the uneven line lengths, the varying number of lines per stanza, and surely the indentations. Then I'm intrigued by the enigmatic title. What does *Them* refer to? The strong declarative sentence that opens the poem answers that question.

I'm also intrigued by the shifting point of view. The poem begins with first person plural *we*, but in stanza 2 shifts to third person singular *he*, though it seems clear that the speaker is the other half of the *we*. How skillfully the poet handles that shift.

Apparently, the speaker and her partner have come to the track. As she watches him run, she meditates on the trees they have decided to love. She describes those trees in stunning images, similes, and metaphors, e.g., the trees are like *nerves pulled from the body*, a *sliver of Einstein's brain blown up under the microscope*, and *mute women*.

The poet also effectively uses personification. The trees have hair and hands. They wave and suck air. This figure makes the scene dynamic.

Notice, also, the poet's use of repetition. The word *wave* is repeated five times and appears in each stanza except stanza 2. This gives the poem a musical cadence and adds motion to the scene.

Begin your poem with this line: "We have _____ to _____ _____."

Fill in the first two blanks with verbs and the last one with a noun. For example, you might have *We have vowed to defend bees* or *We have pledged to consume chocolate*.

Pick up from your first line and freewrite for 10-15 minutes.

As you revise, try to use these strategies:

1. Switch from *We* to *He* (or *She*) at some point.
2. Select a key verb and repeat it five times.
3. Personify the subject of the poem, i.e., whatever you have named at the end of your first sentence.
4. Include at least three strong images, similes, and/or metaphors.

After you have taken the poem through multiple drafts and feel that you are close to done, break the poem into stanzas and arrange the lines into an artistic pattern of indentations. Remember: Do not do this early in your drafting as doing so might tempt you to make your poem fit the form. Instead, find the form that fits the poem.

Sample Poems

We Have Walked to Praise Willows

Like we do,
    these trees circle Harlem Meer,
      wild-haired girls leaning into lake
        to admire their own reflections.

He watches their lanky arms sway in lazy breeze,
    verdant bowers wild against cobalt.
      He steps from the path, freeing
        stagnant October leaves into piles of sunbeams.

Then against vellum moon he throws handfuls
    trying to catch a few
      that weave and fall back
        like drunken fireflies.

Still as midnight,
    I'm stuck to the path.
      He tosses
        a handful my way.

Breaking one hosanna-thin branch—
    two leaves caught like minnows
      on a single hook—
        he presses it into

my wild, hungry hand.

—Linda Simone

To Ride the Waves

We vowed to ride the waves
      and not go under after, on our honeymoon,
you swam out beyond the breakers,
      until the rip tide carried you too far, and
          the lifeguard rose to stand on his chair—

we vowed to ride the waves toward
      shore, never to venture too far out again, never
again to see our heads like small black dots,
      distant bits of flotsam or jetsam—
          punctuation marks in the long story

of the sea. He told me he was a strong
      swimmer, vowed he could hold his own
against any tide, but he was wrong, and
      though he made it back to shore that day,
          another fiercer tide took him away, across

the bar, beyond the skill of any guard on
      sea or land. We vowed before the altar to be true
      until death do us part, and kept that vow
          but now he floats, not dead man's but
          beyond all reach while I still ride the waves.

      —Penny Harter

The Poet on the Poem: Susan Rich

Blue Grapes

There are days made entirely of dust
months of counter-winds

    and years unbalanced on the windowsill.

The soup poured in the same yellowed cup.

Newspapers appeared like oracles on your doorstep—
gilded fragments of anonymous love.

    You stayed in bed, read novels, drank too much.

God visited, delivered ice cream; returned your delinquent library books.

Is it simpler after you're dead
to watch the living like characters on an old-fashioned TV set?

    The dying are such acrobats—

You see them ringing doorbells with their clipboards
remarking on the globes of lilacs.

    They try to lure you out; request a drink of water,
some blue grapes. This does not work.

    Then the dying leave you to yourself—

to the girl dressed in black, suffused with commas,
and question marks—

    How to write your one blue life?

DL: I'm intrigued by the form of your poem. You alternate 2-line and 1-line stanzas. Then you also alternate lines that are flush to the left margin with lines that are indented several spaces. How did you arrive at this form?

SR: I believe this poem needs the freedom to move across the page; it needs to wander. My reason for the indentations and alternations is that for me, and perhaps for my readers, the oddness of the subject—God delivering ice cream, for example—is best represented with a physical shape that quietly signals a slightly different type of poem, different from straight narrative. Or perhaps my reason for this choice is as simple as this: when I open a journal, my eye is immediately attracted to the poems that frame white space in startling ways.

In "Blue Grapes" I wanted to explore an interior, surreal landscape of loss. This unreliable, yet definite pattern emerged. At first, I was afraid that this wasn't a poem. It arrived in fragments and I was unclear about how the parts would fit together.

I write the first few drafts of a poem in red notebooks with graph paper. My process is often very messy—this form was my way of trying to honor the messiness of thought.

DL: Punctuation seems important in this poem. You violate Richard Hugo's prohibition against the semi-colon, you pepper the poem with em dashes, you make reference to *commas, / and question marks*, and you include two questions. Tell us your thoughts about the role of punctuation in the poem.

SR: When I was in elementary school in Massachusetts, in the late 1960's, there was little emphasis placed on correct punctuation; instead, the teachers encouraged full expression. Students chose which books we wanted to read for our curriculum and we created our own poetry anthologies. Fortunately or unfortunately, this means that since I did not learn the hard and fast rules of punctuation when I was young, I sometimes get into trouble when I am writing. It also means my ideas on punctuation remain fluid.

And yes, I do have a great fondness for the em dash. I'm amazed that it isn't used more in poetry. Punctuation, like poetry, remains a bit like magic to me. So often poets seem to let go of punctuation in their poems. I prefer to use different punctuation marks for my own strange purposes. I recall Denise Levertov's strict guidelines for how long to pause after a comma and how long to stop at the end of a line. Many of Levertov's poems were set to music, yet she was never satisfied with the scores; they didn't equate with the music she heard in her head. I offer this by way of explanation. I want to use punctuation to score the poems, to make them equate with the music inside my head.

DL: There's a surreal element in the poem. You give us *years unbalanced on the windowsill*, newspapers that appeared *like oracles on your doorstep*, and a God who *visited, delivered ice cream; returned your delinquent library books*. How do you achieve these dreamlike moments? How hard is it to trust them, to allow them into the poem?

SR: Wow, I love this question, but I want to first turn it around. The dream-like moments are the core of the poem; they are the force of the vision I'm trying to express. I think of Elizabeth Bishop saying that what she wants while reading a poem is *to see the mind in motion*. My mind goes to the odd and the unlikely. I've always been interested in the juxtaposition of the quiet of morning coffee with the news of the world. As a child the unfolding of the newspaper from itself taught me that the world was out there waiting for me to try to understand it.

Now to answer your question more directly: these dream-like moments come easily to me; they are the way my mind works, the way I understand the world. I find no tonal separation between the line *you stayed in bed, read novels, drank too much* and the next line *God visited, delivered ice cream; returned your delinquent library books*. In fact, I do not drink alcohol, so that first line seems more preposterous to me. Poetry works as an avenue of presences, a way to live in the world that exists beyond what we can actually know.

DL: The poem includes a line borrowed from poet Deborah Digges: *The dying are such acrobats*. The line appears just beyond the mid-point, but was it the impetus for the poem? Did it ever appear earlier in the poem? Talk about its influence on the poem.

SR: Sometimes when I write, I find myself losing interest in a poem long before it's done—and certainly I do abandon poems. I'm pretty ruthless when it comes to tossing out work. Other times, there's something that I'm caught on—I'm not ready to call it quits, but I don't know where the next handhold is hiding.

In "Blue Grapes" I used Deborah Digges' line to catapult myself back into the work. I was reading and re-reading her book *Trapeze* at the time. The line arrived in the middle of the process. I think of it as the hinge pin to the poem. I worry a little that my favorite line in my poem is not mine at all. And then I remember that most useful quote by T. S. Elliott: *Immature poets imitate; mature poets steal; bad poets deface what they take, and good poets make it into something better, or at least something different.*

I love the sense that I'm able, through my poems, to have a conversation with the poets I admire, especially those who are now deceased. Shortly before I wrote "Blue Grapes," a friend introduced me to the work of Deborah Digges and I became immediately transfixed. Her work gave me permission to try many different approaches to a poem all at once. I hear her voice as strongly lyrical and interspersed with the vulnerability of grief. In a sense, I needed a bit of bravery to continue on with this poem and her line helped me find it.

DL: Beginning with the title, "Blue Grapes," colors play a role in the poem. There's also a *yellowed cup, lilacs*, a *girl dressed in black*, and finally, the *one blue life*. The poem has the feel of a still life painting. Tell us how and why you painted in the colors.

SR: I was deep into studying ekphrastic poetry when I wrote this poem. An emphasis on composition found its way into this piece from the work I was doing on 19th-century women photographers. Another major influence on my poetry is that I teach film studies. I'm constantly asking my students to think in images and symbols, to focus on what is seen.

The irony is that I don't see this poem as colorful or even very cinematic. And yet I can't disagree with you. You've certainly provided solid evidence to prove me wrong! I think my blindness to the poem's colors has more to do with my own understanding of the poem as coming from a supremely interior world. This particular poem felt hard-won. I'm not writing about an event or an easily identifiable feeling here. Instead, I'm trying to pry open my own sense of consciousness. What does it mean to live as a *self*?

I'm not one to write about my own life and this speaker is not me. However, I am very fond of ice cream.

Bonus Prompt: The Borrowed Line Poem

Dip into a poem by someone else and snatch a line that you like. The line should be at least five words long.

On a blank piece of paper or document, write each word of that borrowed line down the right side of your page, one every other line.

Now write your way into a new poem using those words as the line endings for the poem. Continue writing into the open lines that have no borrowed words.

Once you get a draft that you're fairly satisfied with, return to the borrowed words and substitute each one with a synonym. This step may open up new possibilities for your poem.

Play with line breaks.

V. Enhancing Sound

Poetry is composing for the breath.

—Peter Davison

Craft Tip #13: Sing It One More Time Like That: Anaphora

—Ada Limon

I grew up watching soap operas after school. I'd watch them when my older brother would let me and when no one else was home. I knew it was bad acting. I knew that it was designed to be emotionally manipulative. But I was 12 and I wanted to be manipulated. I knew what was coming and it was satisfying.

My favorite part of soap operas was that overdramatic moment when a character would slowly say the same line twice. *I will be back*, Jack from *Days of our Lives* would say, and then repeat, *I will be back*. When it happened, I liked to say it along with him, make a fist and laugh.

Even though I have written songs, and I love writing lyrics, my favorite part of most songs is the chorus, the part of the song that repeats. When I'm driving on some road I've never been on before and listening to a song I've never heard, I can still sing along, because that chorus is coming around again.

To speak plainly: I like repetition. I like repetition. The baseline. The steady drumbeat. The part that makes your knees bend and say, *Here we go again*. In truth, I rarely see it in contemporary poetry, but when I do, I nuzzle into the lap of it like a loyal dog. It's a powerful tool and perhaps, like rhyme, it's fallen somewhat out of favor because of earlier misuse. In poetry, and as a rhetorical device, it's called *anaphora*. I like that because it sounds like *euphoria*. I imagine I have *anaphoria* and I am feeling *anaphoric*.

The examples of anaphora that I find the most thrilling are the simple ones. Take, for example, these lines from Muriel Rukeyser's poem "Waiting for Icarus":

> He said he would be back and we'd drink wine together
> He said everything would be better than before
> He said we were on the edge of a new relation

He said he would never again cringe before his father
He said he was going to invent full-time

The poem invokes the song-like quality of a Greek chorus by using the simple anaphora: *He said.* The tiny uncomplicated anchor at the beginning of each line allows the poem a fullness, a superb cadence, and a sense that we are witnessing a new myth in the making. (And, of course, we are: the myth of Icarus told by the woman waiting on the shore.)

In the contemporary poem, "Letter from My Heart to My Brain," by Rachel McKibbens, we see the anaphora acting as a chant, an incantation, a wicked, yet self-soothing song:

It's okay to lock yourself in the medicine cabinet,
to drink all the wine, to do what it takes to stay
without staying. It's okay to hate God today
to change his name to yours, to want to ruin all that ruined you.
It's okay to feel like only a photograph of yourself

Again, it's the simple anaphora that I find the most powerful. Here, the *It's okay* provides the rocking rhythm of someone speaking kindly, or trying to speak kindly to herself. The repetition offers a weight that lets the poem reach outward while still celebrating its marvelous and idiosyncratic voice.

The anaphora can also serve as a way to root the poem in an emotion or to emphasize a state of being, as in Jennifer L. Knox's poem, "We Are Afraid":

We are afraid
of Mississippi. We are afraid
the frogs will disappear.

Here, the repetition builds into such a whirlwind of force that the audience or reader could quite possibly end up in a cold sweat by the end thinking, *I am really afraid, she's right.*

In my experience, there are just two keys for using anaphora successfully: the strength of language and description within the successive clauses and the overall build of the poem. It's easy to let the anaphora take over the whole poem, but it won't work. You can try it, but it won't work. Again, anaphora functions as a drumbeat, a baseline, but it won't work unless the rest of the poem both sings *and* dances.

Even the writers of soap operas know that they can only have a character repeating a line occasionally, and songs can't just be made up of choruses, but when used correctly, repetition can elevate and enhance a poem in unexpected ways. Don't deny yourself the pleasure of repeating yourself. Sometimes it helps you get heard.

Poem and Prompt

Elegy for my husband

Bruce Derricotte, June 22, 1928-June 21, 2011

What was there is no longer there:
Not the blood running its wires of flame through the whole length
Not the memories, the texts written in the language of the flat hills
No, not the memories, the porch swing and the father crying
The genteel and elegant aunt bleeding out on the highway
(Too black for the white ambulance to pick up)
Who had sent back lacquered plates from China
Who had given away her best ivory comb that one time she was angry
Not the muscles, the ones the white girls longed to touch
But must not (for your mother warned
You would be lynched in that all-white town you grew up in)
Not that same town where you were the only, the one good black boy
All that is gone
Not the muscles running, the baseball flying into your mitt
Not the hand that laid itself over my heart and saved me
Not the eyes that held the long gold tunnel I believed in
Not the restrained hand in love and in anger
Not the holding back
Not the taut holding

—Toi Derricotte

An *elegy* commemorates a death. The speaker expresses sorrow and praise and often offers consolation. While traditionally written as a metrical poem, most contemporary elegies dispense with meter and are sometimes written for non-humans.

Derricotte's elegy for her husband is written in free verse, without stanza breaks, without rhyme, and without terminal punctuation. Line by line, the poem consists almost entirely of sentence fragments which seems appropriate in a poem about loss.

Following the colon at the end of line 1, the poet lists what is missed—body, history, relatives, memories. With only a few exceptions, the items are listed as negatives, as what's *no longer there*. This strategy effectively conveys absence and loss. Derricotte adds to the effect by using anaphora, repeating *not the* over and over. This enhances the feeling of loss and creates a relentless drumbeat rhythm.

For your own elegy, select a deceased person as your subject. Or, if you like, feel free to choose something not human, e.g., your dog, a relationship, an era, your youth, your hair.

Brainstorm a list of the qualities of your subject that you miss. What's gone with the death?

Title your draft "Elegy for _____."

Begin your poem, drawing from your list.

Use anaphora to add structure and rhythm.

Work against your formal impulses—no metrical pattern, no end rhyme.

Use uneven line lengths. This is a difficult challenge for those of us who like symmetry, but do it anyhow.

Dare to use sentence fragments. Try dispensing with terminal punctuation.

Sample Poems

Elegy for Jules

No longer the hard arc of childhood loss
we spoke of at Manhattan lunches
year after year,
you never forgetting
the father who abandoned you in the small New Jersey town,
growing up poor, the shame it took
all your life to make up for,
sophistication your métier whether ballet
or cultivation of the rich you privately excoriated—
hypocrisy or anger unleashed?—
no longer the hysterical email
descriptions of your body breaking down
like Kafka's, the writer you most loved
no longer the analysand of fifty years,
words your template,
your story of absence,
repetition compulsion
done.

—Carole Stone

Elegy for a Family Photo Buried in My Desk

There I am, that long-ago girl,
a wilted flower Hank Williams might have loved
had he been in the front hall, yellow flypaper
and its winged black dots limp by the screen door
where family faces, all upturned, glisten

no more. Gone the cousins arranged by height like von Trapp
children on the stairs, its heavy oak banister out of reach.
Gone my aunt's square dance skirts we wore as choir robes, our legs
soldier-braced by the downbeat of Susan's hand

at the piano footing the stairs. We sang *Amazing
Grace, How Great Thou Art,* Russell's high tenor
not yet breaking, his mother's pride now gone
and gone all the indulgent laughter when we false start

three times, our faces urgent and red
with that moment's heat we had not yet learned
to dance around, children stiff inside gingham
dragging a ruffled flounce. All gone.

Gone to Jesus, the house where we sang,
an electric cross flanking its east side.

—Jane Miller

Craft Tip #14: The Sounds of Vowels

—Ava Leavell Haymon

When we poets are writing at our best, our words coming to us in unbroken sequence, we are entranced by our own language. Sound and sense collaborate without our conscious attention. These extraordinary moments of fluency are not limited to poets writing poems. It happens to all speaking humans. To find an example, listen to someone who is absolutely furious. There's that moment when the intention to *make sense* loses some of its stranglehold. Listen to the cascade of speech that begins when the angry speaker loses control of what is being said and starts to sputter or smash the glassware. Curse words, rhythm patterns, truth, accusations, insulting metaphors flow out without pause or plan. The logic is garbled, but sound and sense align to communicate. We understand the speaker's meaning through our senses as well as our reason. And the sound itself, well, it's often near genius.

How do we lure into our poems even more of this innate expressiveness? How do we ensure that the sound our words create communicates as directly as the sense our words are creating? In my own case, this kind of language is most likely to occur in the stretches of first draft that come effortlessly. These might be as brief as a three- or four-word phrase. We all know we can't—mustn't—keep craft and evaluation in mind during the writing of an early draft. Much later, however, when we are revising, how can we enable that visceral communication to widen into more of the poem?

I have learned to trick myself, but I must use specific strategies. One that my adult students find useful is something I learned from a choir director, an exercise in silencing all consonants. Meaning, in the ordinary sense, disappears, leaving only the sounds of vowels.

The first time you try it, it's impossible. But the knack comes quickly. Practice on a line that's a proven success, such as the old slogan, *Things go better with Coke.* Leave out the consonants, and the slogan becomes, *i Oh eh-ur i Oh.* Say it that way, with the rhythm and inflection that you'd naturally give the original sentence. Reading it normally, you probably accent the line this way: *THINGS go BEH-ter with COKE*, which means you are reading the vowels *i oh / eh-ur i / OH.*

Notice that I'm avoiding naming or counting the feet. Applying critical vocabulary and analysis is the worst thing we could do in this exercise. Continue repeating the line, vowels only, until you begin to forget the meaning and begin to hear it as pure sound. In the pure sound sequence, we hear the repetition of the *i oh*, the rhythm, the way the line prepares us to accent and hold the last syllable. We begin to understand why that slogan stayed on the air for so long.

Get the knack of leaving out the consonants, using this famous slogan. Then use it with the lines in your poem that are not working. It will distract your attention from what you are trying so hard to say and will help you listen to the pure sound with your innate ear, the way a child would. Sometimes, this will enable you to hear where the sound is dull, and often, surprisingly, once we find that spot, we have found where the words do not express all that we intend.

While revising, I'll often think, *It doesn't sound right.* I don't realize that my complaint is literal: my ear does not like the way the poem sounds, no matter how much it pleases my intellect. If this is what you are saying about a draft of your own, read the section of your poem that does not sound right, and pronounce its vowels only. Read it that way, and listen.

I can't promise that this strategy will give you the words you want, but it may help you isolate the precise point at which the poem is failing. You may like what your poem is saying, but pretend you are reading it to a baby and to a native Czech speaker who has never heard English spoken. That's an audience that will hear the sounds alone. I submit that the poem has not done its job until they are intrigued by it, too. The trick is magic, and the magic is this: where the vowels go dull or clunky, that's often where the meaning also flags.

Poem and Prompt

Aria

What if it were possible to vanquish
All this shame with a wash of varnish
Instead of wishing the stain would vanish?

What if you gave it a glossy finish?
What if there were a way to burnish
All this foolishness, all the anguish?

What if you gave yourself leave to ravish
All these ravages with famished relish?
What if this were your way to flourish?

What if the self you love to punish—
Knavish, peevish, wolfish, sheepish—
Were all slicked up in something lavish?

Why so squeamish? Why make a fetish
Out of everything you must relinquish?
Why not embellish what you can't abolish?

What would be left if you couldn't brandish
All the slavishness you've failed to banish?
What would you be without this gibberish?

What if the true worth of the varnish
Were to replenish your resolve to vanquish
Every vain wish before you vanish?

—David Barber

Even just reading this poem silently on the page, you can hear its music. Barber makes bold use of sound devices:

1. End rhyme with a single sound—*ish*—as well as some double rhymes—*vanquish* and *vanish*, *lavish* and *ravish*, *brandish* and *banish*.

2. Internal rhyme—*wishing* and *vanish*, *foolishness* and *anguish*, *peevish* and *sheepish*.

3. Near rhyme—*ravish* and *ravages*, then *self* and *wolfish*, *everything* and *relinquish*.

4. The last word of each line in stanza 1 is repeated as the last word of one of the lines in the last stanza. That's another kind of echo and a tidy way to end the poem.

5. Anaphora is amply used—*What if, All this, All these.*

Note, also, that the poem consists entirely of questions. Not a single declarative sentence in there. This affects the way you read the poem. Your voice rises at the end of each question.

Notice the format of the poem, how it is neatly formatted into triplets.

Finally, notice that each line contains 9-10 syllables. This, too, affects the rhythm of the poem.

Your challenge is to write a poem that meets or attempts to meet the following criteria:

1. repeats the same sound at the end of each line

2. contains some double rhymes—maybe some triple rhymes!

3. contains some internal rhyme

4. contains some near rhyme

5. consists entirely of questions—maybe your title could be an answer?

6. uses anaphora

7. repeats ending words of stanza 1 as ending words in the last stanza

8. formatted as couplets, triplets, or quatrains

You might want to consider words that end with *-ful, -tion, -ed, -age, -ous, -ism, -ent.*

Sample Poems

One More Passage, One More Voyage

Where's the signage to encourage?
Will you help me cast our sortilege,
hope we salvage a fair anchorage?

Do you dare confront our dotage?
Will you help me sort the spoilage?
What's a marriage if not mileage?

Who'd have envisaged this assemblage
back when we foraged, travelled steerage?
Which is wreckage, which is luggage?

Will you rummage through the garage?
Will you help me with the triage?
Will you balance worth and usage?

Where's the roughage you have ravaged,
broken birdcage, wheel-less carriage?
Which the hostage? Which the homage?

What's the image beyond this pillage—
quaint the village, glowing the foliage?
How do we portage the rest of our baggage?

Will you help me trust in sortilege?
Will you read to me the signage?
Will you be my courage, my anchorage?

—Lisken Van Pelt Dus

Seekers

Why do we find the stars miraculous—
their glow fabulous, their draw so luminous ?
What if the stars are much too numerous
for us to count, the universe too perilous?
What if our curious craving is too cavernous.
our needs ravenous, our wanderlust ruinous?
Our ambitious chorus much too egregious
for us to mount tenacious Taurus?
Will the tedious effort be too laborious
if our pious conscience becomes dubious?
Will we find ourselves joyous or incredulous
if we encounter something truly wondrous ?
Will we forever find the universe so miraculous—
the darkness, the stars, their draw still luminous?

—Gloria Amescua

Craft Tip #15: Stressing Stresses

—William Trowbridge

Many aspiring poets seem to assume that, since they're writing *free* verse, they don't need to pay much attention to syllable stresses. That's just for formalists, they think. As Paul Fussell noted long ago in his brilliant *Poetic Meter and Poetic Form*, free verse should be understood in the same way we understood *free world* during the cold war—free, sort of.

Syllable stresses are part of the language, so you can't be free of them. They're going to play a role in the poem, often an important one. And if you don't pay attention to them, they can get very uncooperative. So I encourage aspiring poets to learn to scan a poetic line and to make scansion a regular part of their writing process.

Even though a poem may not be written in a regular meter, metrical effects are still possible, ones that ought to match the sense of a line in a way parallel to Pope's dictum that *the sound must seem an echo to the sense*. So must metrical effects. Here are some free verse examples, with x to mark strong stresses and o for weak.

Notice how looping anapests support the sense of reeling and rolling in Ted Kooser's "Looking for You, Barbara":

```
o   x   o   o   x   o   o   x
the steering wheel turned through my hands
o   o   x   o   x
like a clock. The moon
o   x o  o  x  o  o  o   x
rolled over the rooftops and was gone
```

Think of what would be lost if the poem didn't have that metrical effect.

Now note how putting heavy stresses together helps give the sense of Ken's Neanderthal thickness in Denise Duhamel's

"Kinky" as Barbie tries to exchange heads with him by pulling hers

```
       X  O    X    X    O    X    X   O    O    X    X   O    X   O
       over  Ken's bulging neck socket. His wide jawbone jostles/
```

And then Duhamel shifts to dactyls to make us feel the rhythm of

```
       X    O    O    X    O   X  O  O    X
       one of those nodding novelty dogs
```

```
       X   O    O   X    O    O    X    X    O    O  X
       destined to gaze from the back windows of cars.
```

In "The Oracle at Delphi, Reincarnated as a Contemporary Adolescent Girl," Amy Gerstler bunches weak stresses to support the gas image:

```
   X  OO  O XOO   XO   X     O   O X O X O  X   X
   Dizzying invisible gasses leaked from my hello kitty backpack
```

And look how Andrea Hollander, in "Giving Birth," uses bunched strong stresses to help convey the ordeal of childbirth:

```
       O    O   X     X    X    O  X   O    X
       On your back, heels locked in metal straps
```

and then moves into smooth iambics when she describes some tranquil villagers to whom she compares the subject's previous life. They are

```
       X  O   O X    O   X O  X O X O    X   O   X
       going about their daily repetitions, looking up.
```

It's not unusual to find a free verse poem shifting into or toward iambics to augment a sense of closure. You even find William Carlos Williams doing it sometimes. This advocate of modernism and proponent of free verse knew the value of stressed syllables.

Next time you write a poem, put those stresses to work.

Poem and Prompt

Wind in the Ozarks

It files and defiles.
It pounds at the door in the dead of night.
It plays odd chords on the shed's warped slats.
It cries like a child in an upstairs crib.
It scurries and scratches in the wall.
It whines. It flakes the paint.
It curls the roof's tin edge.
It peels the snow in tendrils off the bluff.
It loosens a crack in the rock, worrying it like a tooth.
It is a mallet, a sledge.
It dents and chisels.
It scuffs the pond's clear lens.
It whips the bungied, flapping tarp off the woodpile
and lets the rain soak in.
It seeks the hearth where the damp logs hiss and pop,
and drifts like a spirit down the flue.
It moans the embers' long collapsing sigh.
It frays the curtain. It tatters the web.
It scours the glass with a flung fistful of grit.
It rips and tears. It jimmies the catch.
It pries the window with a blade like a knife.
It covers the tracks of the thief.
It rattles. It batters.
It seeps and ekes.
It finds the candle in a shuttered room
and slants the wax across the nub.
It whistles. It hums. It baits
the moon's brass hook with a cloud
and trolls the hills
for the dark that will swallow us whole.

—Davis McCombs

143

The reader's eye is immediately drawn to this poem's odd form with its alternating line lengths, some short, some long, and, of course, the unusual way the entire poem is pushed (blown?) to the right margin.

Then as soon as you read the poem, you feel its force. Read it aloud and you'll feel its power even more. McCombs chooses an ordinary enough topic, but energizes it with a variety of techniques.

One such techniques is figurative language. Using personification, the poet animates the wind, giving it human qualities: it *pounds, moans, finds, whistles, hums,* and *trolls.* McCombs also uses several similes to describe what can't be specifically described. The wind *cries like a child in an upstairs crib.* It *loosens a crack in the rock, worrying it like a tooth.* It *drifts like a spirit* and *pries the window with a blade like a knife.*

Strong verbs also add to the poem's power: *whips, scuffs, frays, rips, tears.* These verbs often appear as compounds. The poem opens with a good example: *It files and defiles.* Line 5 has another: *It scurries and scratches in the wall.* Later, *It dents and chisels.* This device adds rhythm and action and doubles the wind's force.

Notice the array of sound devices. Anaphora is used throughout the poem as almost every line begins with *It* followed by a verb. Notice, also, the use of monosyllabic words: *It curls the roof's tin edge* and *It scuffs the pond's clear lens.* The predominance of hard sounds gives the wind a hammering effect: the *p* in *pounds, plays, paints, pops, whips, flapping*; the *k* in *chords, crib, curls, flakes.*

Finally, McCombs puts meter to work, including lots of iambic feet as in *It whines. It flakes the paint* and *It seeps and ekes.* Several lines mingle iambic feet with anapestic ones, e.g., *It plays odd chords on the shed's warped slats* and *It frays the curtain. It tatters the web.*

For your new poem first choose something from Nature as your topic. Perhaps the sun, lightning, the ocean, a tornado, lava, a blizzard. Make your choice specific to a location as McCombs makes wind specific to the Ozarks.

Before you begin drafting, spend a few minutes generating a long list of powerful verbs that might be used with your subject.

As you begin your first draft, incorporate some of the techniques that McCombs uses. Try some personification, similes, anaphora, monosyllabic words, and words with strong sounds. Get in those verbs and be sure to pair up some of them.

In your revision, consider rhythm. If you're not comfortable with meter, simply go through your lines and notate the stressed and unstressed syllables. Where you have a string of unstressed syllables, revise for better sounds.

Experiment with alternating line lengths.

Several revisions down the road, consider how you might format your poem so as to reflect or imitate your subject. Remember that you're not married to the left margin.

Sample Poems

Mojave Summer

Provoked by human audacity, Sun races over Sunrise Mountain
summoning wind to bellow and shriek its outrage.

Sun's fire incinerates weak grass, sucks its green,
leaves dead brown shafts.
Incensed by streets over its sand, Sun draws fire from the earth's core,
and radiant heat melts our black streets till
they soften, burning bare feet and sandal soles.

Wind slams giant billboards, flipping them
into buildings, like a deck flung wide in a 52-pickup game.
Sand, thrashed into a frenzy, invades stores, homes, offices,
thrusts through cracks, falters and falls,
litters shelves, tables, dressers, lamps, books.
"Close the piano cover!" cries Mother.

Sun, inflamed with violence, roasts hair,
broils shoulders and skin.
Even closed eyes are no defense;
heat burns through eyelids, chopping into the brain.

Desert summer's savage attack weakens,
its mad clamor spent as wind races away—
to bowl rocks over sand, rip out mesquite and cacti,
while lizards, snakes, birds and bobcats hide.
Sun gives way to dark warm night.

—Jane West

Shapeshifter

I'm prodigiously prolific vulnerable venerable invincible
I'll feed you rest you tease you haunt you never taunt you

I'll cleanse you collect you cheer you never leer at you I'm
your innocence your fears I'll surround sound confound you

I'm your prime timer the primitive primeval mover I can keep
you wondering over me until the end of your days and for all

of my nights I'm as faithful as faithful can be you can munch
me up for brunch and I'll crunch you down for lunch I'll circle

your neck sit between your toes slide down your throat and silly
up your nose I'll never disown you I will drown you whenever

you're ready turn and return to me come back for all seasons
I'm the biggest pappymammy before the first I was the first

I'm all my snow springs clouds creeks rivers rain lakes
dew fog ice waterfalls I'm your blood semen milk tears urine

saliva sweat I'm seven tenths you ten tenths of you and
before the last I will be the last I'm the grandest swell of swells

fastest fattest I'm great green gobs of ocean gut belly
willing able to cover you with tidal tucks walk into me walk

into me walk into me while remembering me while touching
while seeing while smelling while tasting while hearing me

you name me ocean all ocean all shining ocean
ocean shunning none all shining shunning none Ocean

—Maren Mitchell

The Poet on the Poem: Robert Wrigley

Earthquake Light

March 11, 2011

Earlier tonight an owl nailed the insomniac white hen.
She'd fluttered up onto a fence post to peer at the moonlight,
to meditate in her usual way on the sadness of the world

and perhaps the hundreds of vanished eggs of her long life here.
I was watching from the porch and thinking she ought not to be
where she was, and then she wasn't, but taken up, a white hankie

diminishing in the east, one the owl would not ever drop.
Now an hour after, the new night wind spins up a leghorn ghost
of her fallen feathers, under the moon and along the meadow grass.

Corpse candle, friar's lantern, will-o'-the-wisp chicken soul
dragging its way toward me, that I might acknowledge her loss
and her generosity, and wonder again about her long-standing

inability to sleep on certain nights. There are sky lights
beyond our understanding and dogs whose work it is to scent
the cancer no instrument can see. On the nights she could not sleep,

the hen Cassandra Blue perched herself with a clear view to the west
and studied the sky, every two seconds canting her head a few degrees
one way or the other. What she saw or if she saw it I cannot say,

though it seemed that something, always, somewhere, was about to go
terribly wrong. Then again, it always is. Now there's a swirl
of wind in the meadow, spinning three or four final white feathers

west to east across it, and there's a coyote come foolishly out
into the open, hypnotized by feather flicker, or scent, then seeing
by moonlight the too-blue shimmer of my eyes, and running for its life.

DL: Almost every line of this poem contains some kind of musical device. Line 1, for example, has the internal rhyme of *tonight* and *white*. The *-ight* sound is strewn throughout the poem—*moonlight, night, might*—as are the long *i* words—*Life, friar's, I, sky lights, eyes*. There's also a good deal of assonance and alliteration in the poem. Tell us how you created this network of sounds.

RW: Well, there's no formula; there's no scheme or discernible pattern. It's just writing via sound linkages. My poems, generally at least, work toward sonic unity. As much as anything else, this is the way I learned to make poems, allowing the sounds of individual words and syllables not only to unify the poem but even to determine its progress.

Richard Hugo, who was one of my teachers, always said, when the poem requires a decision between music and meaning, always pick music. This doesn't mean that meaning should not matter; poems mean, but *how* they mean is vastly more important than *what* they mean. *Picking music* allows the poem's language to conceive itself into being. And it forces the poet to employ all available resources in order to make the conceptions of the language cohere. In this regard, the sound of the poem, as Frost would have said, is the sense.

I might also say that I have a particular fondness for the musical power inherent in long vowel sounds. Consonants are mostly percussive, and I love percussion. But vowels are notes. Balancing vowels and consonants is the way we make our music on the page.

DL: Talk about your long lines. Did you write this poem in long lines or revise into them?

RW: I write line by line. Always do. And I have to have some sense of the line, however loose it might seem to someone else, in order to see how the poem might move on. As with the sounds of the words, I let lines—and, therefore, line breaks—help determine the poem's progress toward a unified structure. I can't recall ever trying to make the first line of this poem be anything but a longish (15 syllables in all) declarative sentence. And that declaration demands elaboration.

The verb *nailed*, and the adjectives *insomniac* and *white* are where the poem's complexity is begun. *Nailed*, in this context, is a kind of vernacularism for *gotten* or, in the case of the hen, *killed*, although it may also be said that Japan was itself nailed by the March 11, 2011, earthquake. *White* is pretty ordinary, adjectivally-speaking, but it comes into substantial play in the totality of the poem's imagery. The natural symbolic values of white are exactly what they are. *Insomniac* is the ringer; at least it was for me in the writing. Chickens don't usually have trouble sleeping, but animals have mysterious skills and sensitivities. Thus the cancer-sniffing dogs later on.

Once I had the first line, I felt the rhythmical contract was established, so most of the subsequent lines have a similar length, both in terms of syllables and stresses. This is also a unifying strategy. Like Frost, I believe the poem is (perhaps even *must be*) a momentary stay against confusion.

DL: I've noticed that you have an affection for symmetrical verses, i.e., stanzas with the same number of lines and fairly even line lengths. What made you choose 3-line stanzas for this poem?

RW: I like the challenge of regularizing, of building stanzas that are symmetrical and whose construction comes to be a necessary component of how they get said what must be said; that's just one way of increasing the degree of difficulty in the work of writing. And I've always been of the opinion that increasing the degree of difficulty formally or structurally is part of the process of deepening the poem's complexity.

The difficulty of the art is what addicts us to its creation, after all. We become infatuated with the possibilities of that difficulty, the challenge of the problem of the poem's writing. I do see, looking back at earlier drafts, that, as I closed in on a final draft, the poem was first in six quatrains. Meaning the opening quatrain ended with a period, with *her long life here*. This would also have been when I noticed the effect of organizing the poem into tercets instead, so that *sadness of the world* is both the end of a line and the end of the first stanza. That stanza break allows the opening stanza's final phrase to ring a bit longer, and what else is the poem about but the sadness of a world in which there is often no running for your life—not from owl, earthquake, or fate.

DL: I see another kind of symmetry in this poem, one of content. Tell us about the parallel between the owl and the hen introduced in the first stanza and the coyote and the speaker in the last stanza, the link between *Cassandra Blue* and the *too-blue shimmer* of the speaker's eyes, and the shared sleeplessness.

RW: The owl is not malign; it's just an owl. The coyote, like the owl a predator, is drawn by the scent of potential prey, but it sees the eyes of the speaker in the moonlight, and sensing danger runs off. The *too-blue shimmer* is a play on blueness, depression, which both the speaker and the hen are afflicted by, for some reason. That the owl's named *Cassandra* suggests that her sleeplessness has something to do with a gift (or more likely a curse) for prophecy, even if she knows only that something bad is about to happen. The unspoken presence, of course, is the earthquake, which is also not malignant but *merely* catastrophic. If there is a greater curse than knowing what will happen, I can't imagine what it might be. And yet, the catastrophe that befalls the hen is not something, despite her Cassandra-like gift, she can foresee. Unless it is, which is all I think I can say, without saying too much.

DL: Your poem has several metaphors for the dead hen: *white hankie, leghorn ghost, Corpse candle, friar's light, will-o'-the-wisp.* Do you have a method for getting your brain to unleash these metaphors? Were there any that had to be omitted?

RW: Most of them are synonyms for one another: *corpse candle* and *friar's light* being more or less the same thing as *will-o'-the-wisp. White hankie* is a kind of remembrance, and *leghorn ghost,* for better or worse, is a chickenish image. But the speaker's role in the poem to this point is thoroughly passive; he's a witness to the hen's pondering and to her being killed. When this onslaught of figures comes in, he's still sitting on the porch, but he's active in his imaginative re-seeing, a re-seeing that is an endeavor to understand not only what he has seen and continues to see, but, as it turns out, what he will come to know the larger significance of.

DL: Your title is simple but elegant and inviting. Nevertheless, I wonder about its connection to the poem. The dating of the poem suggests some connection to the earthquake that occurred on that date in Japan, but the poem is clearly not set in Japan. Is this another kind of metaphor?

RW: The title came first. This is, almost always, a terrible thing for me. I was probably looking up something else, in a book or online, when I came across the phrase *earthquake light*, and an explanation thereof. It's a real thing—mysterious, abundantly theorized upon, and even challenged as myth. There have been many reports of peculiar, seemingly sourceless lights in the sky at or near to areas of extreme seismic activity. That such a phenomenon is not explainable but has been witnessed captured me immediately. The mystery of it appeals to me and I have this sense that there is a similar mystery attendant to the best poems. It's not just in what gets said but in how it gets said, and that sort of mystery is mythic, bardic, and endlessly sweet to me.

The poem was composed within a few months of the Tohoku earthquake. My wife has had dreams of things happening before they've happened. I've had one or two. There is something as alive in the earth's soul as there is in a poem. That kind of mystery, I mean, in which an insomniac hen may well be aware of or even foresee a catastrophic happening on the other side of the planet. Or perhaps in the vast nervy continuum of chickendom, a Japanese bantam beheld an otherworldly light in the sky, just before the earth itself moved.

Much as I confess I love the word *chickendom*, I also have to say that I'm honestly and deeply attuned to animals. There's nothing misanthropic in that. I simply have come to admire the way most animals, especially wild animals, are at ease within their own skins in ways most human beings never are. Of course, Cassandra Blue is both domesticated and anthropomorphized. It may be that her sadness is in that.

Bonus Prompt: Accentual Verse Poem

Accentual verse has a fixed number of stresses per line regardless of the number of syllables present. The poet is free to determine both the fixed number of stressed syllables and the total number of syllables in the line.

The poem "what if a much of a which of a wind," by E. E. Cummings, is an example of accentual verse. In the following lines from the poem, the number of accents in each line is consistently four while the number of syllables varies from seven to ten. The accented syllables are indicated in boldface.

> **what** if a **much** of a **which** of a **wind**
> **gives** the **truth** to **sum**mer's **lie**;
> **blood**ies with **dizz**ying **leaves** the **sun**
> and **yanks** immor**tal stars awry**?

Choose a subject for an accentual poem, perhaps a headache, a fear, the ocean, fireworks, or anything else that appeals to you.

Write one line of accentual verse giving that first line four accented syllables.

Pick up from that first line. Pursue your subject and maintain the pattern of four accents per line.

As you become proficient at accentual verse, you may want to challenge yourself to create a pattern of alternating numbers of accents per line. For example, the odd lines might have five accents while the even lines have six.

VI. Adding Complication

Poetry is the dark side of the moon. It's up there,
and you can see the front of it.
But what it is isn't what you're looking at.
It's behind what you're looking at.

—Charles Wright

Craft Tip #16: Putting Obstructions Along Your Poem's Path

—Fleda Brown

The mind—my mind—has its grooves. It's been perfectly happy, thank you, with the routes it's carved over the years. If I want the poem to surprise anyone, I must, as Frost said, surprise myself first. But how can I do that when basically everything that enters my mind heads out along its predictable pathway before I catch conscious hold of its thread?

What are poetic forms but planned obstructions, arbitrary rules that make words stumble, make us go in a direction we hadn't intended? What is a dance but a deliberate interruption of the body's prosaic movements? Ellen Bryant Voigt recommends *structural subversion*. I recommend, and employ, any sort of subversion I can come up with.

I think of everything I can do to make myself clumsy. When I stumble, I'm likely to see, low to the ground, a hidden alcove, a secret passage. Once I have some words on paper, some draft to work with, no matter how fuzzily conceived, I can begin setting up barriers for myself.

Consider casting any of these obstructions along your poem's path:

1. How many perfect words have arisen because of the need to make a rhyme? Follow a strict rhyme scheme, even if you invent it yourself. Let it drive the poem far from where you began. Let it make the poem insanely wrong, if necessary. Do not deviate from it until you're entirely satisfied with this rhymed poem. Then feel free to break it apart. There may be a better/different poem inside.

2. Follow a strict meter. Or a strict syllable count. Or invent an entire form with patterned line breaks.

3. Once you have something going, some inclination in a poem, pick a book of someone else's poems. Choose a book

whose poems draw you at the moment. Go through it and make a list of more than a dozen words that appeal to you. Make yourself use them in your poem. Since you already have your mind on the poem, the words you choose will magically relate, one way or another.

4. Do not let yourself write more than four lines moving in the same direction. Turn a corner; see what's behind the curtain; recall a moment in childhood. Recall your aunt Millie washing a pot of exactly the same color as the blue you've just seen in a bird's wing. Don't worry if the connection is tenuous. You can revise later if you need to.

Some stumbling blocks work for some poems, others for other ones.

What I want to emphasize here is the need for the kind of awareness that comes from preventing a *natural flow*. Or, rather, not preventing it, not that, but after the flow has happened, going back and building an obstruction against the clichés your mind latches onto. Think about what happens when water's dammed up. It gets quieter, the silt settles, and you can maybe see all the way to the bottom. My goodness, there's a pike down there, as still as if it were sealed in amber. Farther down, shadows, a sunken boat, sunken tires. What of that? What is opening before your eyes?

Poem and Prompt

The Hospital of His Wounds

I take a kind of nourishment from water sizzling in a stream
or autumn leaves boiling in the street as wind stirs the pot.
I am a body sustained by lean meats, consoled as I wait
to see what remains after everything I'll forget
and have forgotten. It will be a natural monument,
like a canyon or mountain, something weathered into existence
by the slow powers of erosion and subterranean pressure.
Although, even now certain gorges and passages take shape.
For instance, that night at about 2:30 a.m., a jagged wailing
as if a newborn had been bludgeoned by a blackjack
startled us from sleep to find a possum in the dogwood
and a raccoon testing his boundaries, like me with memories,
wondering what kingdom they circumscribe, and my role there,
and why I should be tickled to recall your fascination with roadkill,
or why I can't forget a crow that pinned a pigeon
and pecked the meat spilling from a wound in its neck,
and now a headline that has never left me, which read
that a man was "in the hospital of his wounds." I remember
thinking how, by this odd syntax, he would convalesce
in strange pulsing rooms, deep in his lacerations and bruises,
healing at the root of marrow and lava and memory,
halls and corridors that could not be photographed
like anything of real passion but where he would wake
as the first man to know who he was without looking back.

—Michael T. Young

Young's multi-layered poem pulls the reader right in with its double metaphor. The poet likens Nature to *a kind of nourishment* or food, then to a cook as water sizzles, leaves boil, and wind *stirs the pot*. The speaker fuses with Nature as he anticipates becoming *a natural monument*. This leads him back to a memory of having been awakened by the shrieking of animals which he compares to the cries of a newborn being bludgeoned—a horrific but effective image. Now Young skillfully brings in an auditor, someone with a fondness for roadkill. The speaker recalls having seen a crow devour a pigeon from *a wound in its neck*. This leads to the recollection of an odd newspaper headline.

The speaker now imagines a man who enters the hospital of his own body, a hospital with rooms and hallways. Such a man would have no need of memories for he would already know himself in the deepest way possible.

Consider the form and structure of the poem. Its one fat chunk of a stanza makes sense as one metaphor touches off another and one idea leads seamlessly to the next. Metaphors and ideas accumulate and the poem grows increasingly dense. Similarly, the sentences get progressively longer as the poem develops. How cleverly the poet links content, form, and sentence.

Notice, too, the poem's use of sound devices, e.g., the assonance of the repeated long *e* sound in the opening lines: *stream, leaves, street* and the repeated long *a* sound in *sustained, wait, remains, subterranean*. Consonance is also abundant as in the repeated *s* sound in *convalesce, strange, pulsing, rooms, lacerations, bruises*. Finally, alliteration contributes to the poem's music, for example, in the hard-hitting *b* sounds of *been, bludgeoned, blackjack*.

Scour the newspaper or a magazine for an odd, intriguing headline. Do not read the article. Free associate with your headline. Quickly write down your thoughts. To get yourself thinking metaphorically, keep asking yourself, *What does this remind me of* or *What does this look like?*

Now begin the first draft with a few related metaphors (if they don't come now, you can add them later—or not). Let the metaphors lead to a related memory or two. Feel free to make up your memories. Bring in your headline and let it work its magic.

Tip: Don't run away from darkness. Let it enter your poem if your poem calls for it.

As you revise, feel free to change the order of your material. Try working with long lines and progressively longer sentences. Try for a single chunky stanza. Let it be dense.

Then work on sounds. Tune up the poem until its music is something you hear and feel as you read your poem aloud. And do be sure to use oral reading as part of your revision process. Try using a voice recorder.

Sample Poems

Eco-Minded Innovators Disrupt the Rituals of Death

The plants I started from seeds in peat pots
on the kitchen table have withered and died.
Watering requires presence, and I am absent,
more often than not. When I'm not absent,
I'm forgetful, or lazy about the simplest tasks
like opening the tap, filling the can, pouring water,
repeat, repeat, but the electric bill is due and
something is on the television and I am late
for a meeting or didn't take my vitamins
this morning. I revel in distraction while my
next door neighbor prunes his roses daily,
cuts errant grass stalks with a pair
of scissors, removes each fallen leaf. I hate him.
Years ago I grew parsley and snap peas
and California poppies in beds of vermiculite
on the small porch of a tiny apartment. Later
I learned vermiculite damages the lungs,
the irony that its manufacturer is named
Grace. Today the New York Times tells me,
Eco-Minded Innovators Disrupt the Rituals
of Death. Joke's on them. Death makes its
own rules. Dad didn't scatter his ashes,
we did. Look, seeds from last year's rotten
tomatoes sprouted in the yard. They mind
their own business, remain focused,
don't need my help.

—Jessica de Koninck

State of Emergency

The greatest danger comes from within,
the body a tuning fork struck and sounding,
from even the slightest touch of skin against skin or not skin.
In Attawapiskat, where the world draws chilly breaths,
the walls of fishing shanties nothing
but splinters and wind, snowflakes peck the glass
like loose feathers torn from gulls' wings.
The sky is an empty mirror, reflecting cold
pale blues the ocean gave up for adoption.
Here, the state of emergency exists in minds
at war with themselves, alone in their shells,
ghosts of lost First Nation tribes.
I remember the Reykjavik mountains. The desolate expanse of land
stretched beneath them, a long gray-green shadow
of frozen lava flow, the brittle craggy outcroppings
now lined with fluffy mosses, life creeping back into crevices
of a continent wanting only to purge itself of ground zero memories.
Even there the gulls circled and splattered the stone
with their white splotches of guano,
their primitive cries pinging the cliffs.
I understand the dark caul
of isolation, segregating the self
from the unknown beauty of tomorrow, the untaken steps
through unopened doors, where the Earth spreads its arms
and says *breathe me in.* Listen to the song of ice and fire
swelling and receding like water trapped in rock,
cooled and warmed under the moon and the sun.
There's another verse waiting to be sung,
and if you wait for the stillness of the body's return,
the words will rise like steam
from the summit crater of your throat.

—Jay Sizemore

Craft Tip #17: The Poem's Other

—Alberto Ríos

What we are about to do: It is wild, but not lost. It consists of saying exactly, precisely what we do not want to say. It cannot help but make our hearts beat faster as a result. This is new writing that will not behave, but it is ours, absolutely ours, ourselves rediscovered.

Have you ever seen a photographic negative? It is indeed the photo, but in what seems like opposite or reverse light. Think of this as you try the exercise.

1. Begin with a poem you have already finished and which you like.

2. Now, write the opposite of your poem, the poem's other.

3. In creating the poem's other, you will simultaneously be creating your own Other, the other side of yourself, something yours and not yours, connected to you but not you.

4. You may go concept by concept, but try word by word.

5. Use a dictionary and a thesaurus, especially when you get stuck. Look for antonyms.

6. For some things, like *goose* or *spaghetti*, you will wonder what the opposite is. The answer, while it may be subjective, is still there to be found. Don't let the glitches confound you. Find an answer, even when there is none to be found. And whatever you come up with, when the dictionaries and thesauruses and reference books fail you, understand that only you can have invented it. Trust yourself and the moment and the immediacy of whatever offers itself as an opposite.

7. Make this make sense. Don't let the poem slip away from you and get silly. Treat the process with respect, the same way you do when you write a poem in the regular way.

8. Go with and trust the first thing that comes to mind, then move on. Don't second-guess yourself.

9. Don't make any value judgments—no this is good, no this is bad. Just let it be whatever it is. In other words, don't stop yourself by being scared to write something that doesn't sound good to you. Get out of your own way.

10. Don't choose—be guided. Now is not the time to bring new things into the mix, however strong the impulse might be—and it will be. You're an artist, after all, never content with what is. But use that selfsame energy to ride this exercise out to its finish. It, too, looks to change, but its strategy is bigger than the single moment.

11. Again, don't try to force an outcome, or to craft something that is not there. Remember, you have already finished this piece of writing. Rewriting is not what we are doing. We are turning these words around on the page, repositioning them, looking at their facets, giving them depth. We are looking at their other side. Give them their fair chance.

12. Be willing to be surprised, open to whatever will tell itself—whether you like it or not. In other words, let the true other emerge, no matter the consequences.

13. In all this, don't think—react. And keep moving.

14. Most of all, be patient. Follow this through to the end.

The way a photographic negative is also the photograph, this, too, is your poem, your story, your words, but is clearly what you did not want to say or intend to show. It is the opposite. Yin and yang. And there you are. You give to the poem in this moment a life of its own, something that is you but which moves beyond you as well. There's some wisdom in this idea. At the very least, saying what you don't want to say will make you breathe faster, which will offer you something to think about as you gasp. But more than that, it will help you examine what you did, indeed, say, whether you were aware of it or not.

You may think, especially if you really like the poem you've first written, that the outcome will automatically be something you don't like, and perhaps even hate. Getting started may be difficult because of this. The outcome, however, will almost invariably surprise you, and its sudden complexity with regard to what you had originally written will please you, even if it has some edge to it. But this is what you're trying to find, after all, in your writing. At least this is what we say to ourselves.

Poem and Prompt

Changing Genres

I was satisfied with haiku until I met you,
jar of octopus, cuckoo's cry, 5-7-5,
but now I want a Russian novel,
a 50-page description of you sleeping,
another 75 of what you think staring out
a window. I don't care about the plot
although I suppose there will have to be one,
the usual separation of the lovers, turbulent
seas, danger of decommission in spite
of constant war, time in gulps and glitches
passing, squibs of threnody, a fallen nest,
speckled eggs somehow uncrushed, the sled
outracing the wolves on the steppes, the huge
glittering ball where all that matters
is a kiss at the end of a dark hall.
At dawn the officers ride back to the garrison,
one without a glove, the entire last chapter
about a necklace that couldn't be worn
inherited by a great-niece
along with the love letters bound in silk.

—Dean Young

This original and charming love poem seems especially apt coming from a poet. Young creates a comparison between a haiku poem and a Russian novel, a comparison reminiscent of an analogy found on the SAT exam. Here the relationship is small : big. The speaker implies that his former loves could be accommodated in the small space of a haiku, but his new love requires the grand space of a Russian novel.

The analogy is set up in the first three lines of the poem. Line 2 makes two references to images from Basho's haiku and includes the syllable pattern of a haiku. Line 3 begins with *but now*, signaling the turn. This is followed by a generous list of the characteristics of a Russian novel. It seems appropriate that much more attention is given to the Russian novel than to the haiku.

The poem ends with a poignant and romantic image, a perfect way to end the poem and more effective than a statement, a piece of information, or a summary.

Young accomplishes the poem in a mere three sentences.

For your own poem—love poem or otherwise—begin with this starter sentence: "I was satisfied with _____ until _____ but now I want _____."

In the first blank name something small. Follow that with a significant event. Fill in the third blank with something similar to what's in the first but bigger in scale.

For example:
>   cherry tomato : beefsteak tomato
>   sentence : paragraph
>   crumb : cake
>   ginger ale : champagne
>   scoop of vanilla : banana split
>   rain : hurricane

Now brainstorm a list of the attributes of the big item.

Draft the poem, following the *until* _____ with a brief description of your small item. Then follow the turn line with the attributes from your brainstorming list. For the first draft, don't worry about the order of the items.

As you revise, consider if a rearrangement of order might make your poem more effective. Be sure to end with a powerful image.

See if you can limit yourself to three sentences. That's more than a challenge to imitate; it will force you to consider what might be omitted or added, what might be rearranged, where the pace of the poem lags.

For a variation, reverse the relationship in your analogy. Instead of working with small : big, use big : small.

Sample Poems

Ferry Envy

I was satisfied with my rustic curves, the quick capture
and elimination of fish wiggling graffiti into my wood,
until mackerel were traded for children, so many loaded
into me that I sail like a mattress that has been slept on
for too long, sinking in the middle, unable to be shored up
with the cheap fill of corn husks or greasy goose feathers.
Now I want the fiberglass of a ferry, the fierce resistance
to stems and sterns, the cache of kiosks and water closets,
the speed of caffeine and the smug, first-world satisfaction
of consumption. But even my dreams of a dock are mere
delusions of grandeur, castrated on every double return,
and I can only idle, flaccid as seaweed, as the ferries preen
while taking on my cargo in the middle of their lanes, limp
babies sodden with salt water handed up the truncated crosses
of ladders, and blow their own horns three times to signal
reverse thrust as I am towed backwards by my keepers
who come up behind me in speedboats, dragging me up
from under, firing their rifles into the air as if to warn
all who are listening that each time I am robbed and re-chained
it is a celebration, marking me none of their ilk.

—Jen Karetnick

Changing Steps

I loved Zumba—the clipped rhythms
of cha-cha, merengue, salsa, as our Hispanic
teacher shouted to sweating women at the YWCA,
It's all about the "heeps." So I swiveled mine
like the agitator in a washing machine—

until I met a ballroom man and learned to waltz, waltz, waltz
down a long hall—our own Versailles—
rise and fall in a white dress

with its flouncy hem floating—whisks, twinkles, fallaways,
Bocelli crooning *A Mano a Mano,*
Chris and I hand-in-hand

or turn-turn-turning to *Moon River* and its violins: 1-2-3.
I get dizzy if I take my eyes
off the mirror, but dizzy

in a pleasant punch-drunk way, and anyway, he holds me,
leads me with light pressure on my back
and a flick of his wrist—

though I never wanted to be led by a man before, I'd follow him
through slip pivots, développés, and passing changes
in these pink satin heels.

                    —Karen Paul Holmes

Craft Tip #18: Turning a Poem

—Lance Larsen

For a time I served as a first reader of a national poetry competition that draws over 700 book-length manuscripts each year. There were a handful of us, each reading over a hundred submissions and passing along the cream of the cream to the national judge. I had two distinct impressions about the manuscripts that didn't make the cut. First, most possessed an impressive overall competence in execution and verbal nuance. Second, despite many cosmetic virtues, individual poems from these same manuscripts were largely forgettable. By forgettable, I mean they didn't take off the top of my head or make me so cold no fire would ever warm me—Emily Dickinson's litmus test for true poetry. The missing ingredient? Among other things: reversal. That is, a change of scenery, opposition, an altered course, emotional fire. In short, they lacked what nearly any good sonnet possesses: a successful *volta*, or turn.

I'm not advocating that we abandon the poetic pluralism of the current moment in favor of Renaissance fourteen liners that predictably shift direction in line 9 (Italian sonnets) or line 13 (English sonnets). Certainly not all poems need to end in a sestet or a closing couplet. I am advocating that we more consciously incorporate the virtues of the volta in whatever poetry we practice, whether free verse, prose poems, or more avant garde departures.

Sometimes one can learn a great deal about poems by looking elsewhere. Consider this nano short short Hemingway was fond of: *For sale, baby shoes, never worn.* Here we have an entire story in six words, a story that isn't even a sentence, a story whose devastating volta arrives in the last two words. And here's a joke by Woody Allen, whose volta requires the reader to supply a curse that isn't even on the page: *Some guy hit my fender, and I said to him, "Be fruitful and multiply," but not in those words.* Successful turns, whether in narratives, jokes, or aphorisms for that matter, discombobulate the world just a little, flipping the reader into the New.

As you read this very short poem, by Charles Simic, take special note of the strategies used to achieve reversal.

Watermelons

Green Buddhas
On the fruit stand.
We eat the smile
And spit out the teeth.

Or consider Margaret Atwood's 4-line, 2-stanza poem, "You Fit Into Me," in which the speaker hints at a darkly problematic relationship with her lover by reimagining *hook and eye* as a fish hook in an open eye.

I'll mention one final poem, James Wright's "Lying in a Hammock at William Duffy's Farm in Pine Island, Minnesota," which opens with five sentences of observation. Here we have a butterfly, the sound of cowbells, horse droppings blazing up *into golden stones*, the poet himself, and a chicken hawk *float[ing] over, looking for home*. These observations, zen-like in their understated richness, are followed by this unexpected conclusion: *I have wasted my life.* Just when we thought we were safely ensconced in image, Wright opts for declaration, even confession. But call it a confession filled with more questions, which explode a little differently in each reader. This world is no longer that world.

Poems like these three remind us that the world is built on paradox. What the right hand stabilizes, the left hand flicks into disarray.

I've barely scratched the surface here. I hope each reader will reread his or her favorite cache of free verse poems and examine the role of reversal. How many of the poems depend on turns that fly under the radar? And as you examine these examples, I encourage you to think more liberally about the volta, not as a Renaissance workhorse trapped in a 10 x 14 corral (10 syllables x 14 lines) but as a wilder creature of unknown parentage. Let the volta kick a little and snort its impatience, let it wild up the domesticated herd.

Poem and Prompt

A Blessing

To be able to trust your eyes—that's a great blessing.
To believe that the pane of glass in your upstairs window
Is in fact transparent, that the narrow,
Winding streets seeming to lie beyond it
Are not a reflection of something narrow
And dark within you, just a winding passage
That will lead, eventually, to an open square.
To believe you're entitled, when you reach it,
To sit on a bench in the sun by the marble fountain,
That you haven't come to envy the beautiful,
To belittle it, to despoil it. No.
You're here to muse on the possibility
It can serve you as an example,
As a lesson in taking pleasure in what you are,
In giving pleasure by not withholding.
Maybe this gracious self is the person
Your friends have noticed from the beginning.
Your inability to observe it so far
Needn't mean they're deluded, just that their distance
Provides them the chance to see you whole.
Maybe whatever you need to do
To deserve their loyalty you've done already.
If you then do more, it could mean your heart
Has committed itself to overflowing
And you've chosen to let it have its way.

—Carl Dennis

This poem has a meditative quality. The speaker begins with an observation of a simple object—a pane of glass. That leads to reflection and insight about what exists in the interior world of the *you* addressed. Notice how the poet moves the *you* from one place to another, from inside to outside.

Note the use of infinitives to structure the poem, especially in the first half. The infinitive phrases, along with phrases beginning with *that*, appear repeatedly in the first part of the poem. This use of anaphora gives structure and music to the poem and also creates the impression of one thought flowing naturally into the next.

The poem is deceptively simple: plain diction, simple format, and the absence of figurative language until the very end of the poem where the heart is personified. Yet there is a plan at work. The first twelve lines record what is observed. Those lines contain two minor turns, each presented as a negative. The first occurs in line 5 as the speaker tells the *you* that the winding streets are *not a reflection of something narrow and dark within you...*The second occurs in line 10: *That you haven't come...*Then line 13 marks the major turn: *It can serve you as an example...*This turn is followed by another twelve lines, giving us a perfectly balanced poem.

There is a different kind of turn taking place as well. In the first half of the poem, what might be interpreted as a bad sign is turned around and becomes a good sign. The possibility that the *you* might envy what is beautiful and choose to *belittle it, to despoil it* is flipped and becomes a positive opportunity, *a lesson in taking pleasure in what you are,* something that might lead to self-knowledge.

I admire the risks that Dennis takes in the poem. He risks sentimentality but doesn't quite go there. He risks didacticism but his speaker seems more a kindly fellow traveler than a lecturer.

Now onward to your own poem. Let's make it a meditation. And let's see if we can write a happy poem. Let's believe in our potential for good.

Pick a simple object in the room where you are now, something like the window pane used by Dennis. Begin with an infinitive and quickly introduce your object. Use the second person *you* and *your*, and let the infinitives keep pushing the poem forward. Move your person from inside the room to a nearby park or pastoral setting and let him or her spot something else there. Continue the meditation. Let it lead to some kind of self-knowledge or epiphany.

After you have a draft, work on your poem's structure. Aim for the kind of balance that Dennis achieves. Place a turn line right smack in the middle of the poem.

Bonus points for double anaphora, i.e., two phrases that get repeated multiple times.

Sample Poems

Weather Girl

To believe in the tug of a thunderstorm,
the way it pulls eighty years of you up
off the floor. To know that somewhere beyond
the front door of the house, two big dogs
howl while the little dog shivers
under a chair. To find a wren on a twig
tucking its beak to its chest feathers.
To know how it feels to have chest feathers,
a song in your bones that you must sing
during rain and again after rain.
To believe in the tug of a thunderstorm,
how it forms in a hollow sky,
how it outlines the girl you once were,
hollows her out from the rest of you,
calls her back from the dry past,
how the girl runs fast to the hilltop,
spreads her arms like a star, daring
the lightning to kick up her heels.
To yell at the floor you were lying on
when the weather swept in to roll up the rug.
Because the thunderstorm tugs, that's
what it does, and you aren't, no,
you aren't coming home.

—Jenny Hubbard

Blessings at 4 AM

To wake from the old nightmare of returning to work
in a hospital, no one to explain where the orders wait,
what tubes to use to draw blood, a blessing to wake
and to know it's just a dream, not a prophecy or echo
of daytime terrors, my pulse not even quickened.
To rise from bed on legs that function, hardly an ache
to mention, to make coffee and pour a glass of juice,
pantry and freezer full, bills paid, electricity reliable,
clean water at my fingertips, hot and cold. To rise free
of fear of invasions, bombings, carjackings, to know
no one's stalking, no one scrutinizing what I eat or buy
or read or believe. Blessings today when the old
dream says I'm anxious or wounded by the past, and I count
three pets—safe, snoring, warm in bed against me.
The day stretches out like a washed blanket billowing
on a clothesline in the spring breeze, like any whim
might blow me to make art cards in my studio, or beef stew
in a slow oven. No demand to be anywhere, blessed
to be alone and quiet, free to venture out behind the wheel
of a Toyota that whisks me away when desire says, Go!

—Joan Mazza

The Poet on the Poem: Sydney Lea

Blind, Dumb

Ted was the logger, I the greenhorn professor,
Tommy the logger's teenaged son.

I needed distraction, so we took that hike together.
Toward evening a doe crashed past, haphazard.

Ted said, *She's blind.*

She showed as pale as a moose in the dead of winter,
which seemed foreign to me. But then everything did:

the weeks dragged by and my poor wife still lay under
the pall of coma. Our old car had flipped.

I stood and wondered,

how could the doe survive the coming cold?
The full dark loomed, and Tommy pled,

Can't we go for a gun? He didn't want to leave her
to starvation, predation, to that murder of ravens

perched low and bold.

My wife and I had quarreled. She sped away,
blanched by anger I tried to ignore

until the trooper called at the house to say
the Jeep had landed roof-down on Route 4.

On this later day,

the logger appeared to see what I couldn't see:
Not up to us to spare her, he drawled.

My every instinct wanted to disagree,
but as Tommy and I glanced up at the cruel

black birds in the trees,

I was the mute one. Dodging the frantic animal,
we could almost look through her ghostly hide,

scourged bloody by lashes of brush in her scrabbling circles.
Scavengers waited for quarry to die,

sat patient, preened.

I'd read no novel, no poetry that trained
my soul for this—or anything.

So I thought as I felt my uselessness in the scene.
What could I say? What could I do?

My vapid dream

was to start all over again, not having to know
some categorical, unspeakable things.

I'd always imagined words' restorative power,
but I'd witnessed beings who couldn't pass on

what had happened or how.

Words wouldn't help them. To see that so starkly stung.
Speechless, benighted, what had I to teach

a student now, much less a daughter or son?
Frost had unclothed the maple and ash,

so winter could come.

DL: The form of this poem strikes me as a happy marriage between tradition and invention. Tell us how the form evolved.

SL: I recently colluded with the Vermont Contemporary Music Ensemble in a concert; five composers wrote individual pieces that were responses to poems of mine. One of the composers, Erik Nielsen, said that *the hardest part about composition is talking about it.* I identify with such a contention. That said, I have some intuitive answer to your question about form — intuitive because, vague as this inexcusably is, there seems a way in which forms choose me rather than vice versa. More or less strict forms, however unconventional (I rarely use received conventions), are enabling components for me. If I allow myself to play with formal alternatives, I can get away from thinking too hard about what I may *mean.* Paradoxically, that approach allows for such *meaning*—though I mistrust that term—the poem may contain.

In this case, my logger friend—who put small stock in self-revelation via language—imagined that physical exercise would take my mind off the fact that my wife was in a coma. He was wrong, as the poem suggests. I, nonetheless, recalled his good intentions, and the first of the few words he spoke came to mind: *Ted said, She's blind.* A two-stress line. It then occurred to me that most of the important things that would come in the poem would be equally terse; that is, my unconscious told me that, in a poem that has as much to do with the inadequacy of words as anything, the important material would be clipped in that fashion, right up to *so winter could come.* Mind you, I didn't know that would be a line at all, let alone the last; I was, as it were, led there, past *black birds in the trees*, through *my vapid dream*, and so on. The form was built around that inspired keystone.

DL: I deeply admire the wonderful, subtle sounds of your poem. There's some end rhyme, yes, but then there are also rhymes and near rhymes scattered throughout the poem, e.g., *old, cold, bold; called, quarreled, drawled; preened, scene, dream.* How did you make this music happen?

SL: My late friend William Matthews, who was not a formalist like me, once told me in conversation that he tended to like free verse when it sounded most like formal, and vice versa. Me too; hence, the ongoing appeal to me of slant rhyme. And there is my ongoing obeisance to Frost, who, though far stricter in his formal allegiances than I am, still wanted the sound of conversation in his poems. I guess the looseness of my rhyming somehow goes in service of that aim.

DL: Your poem skillfully handles two narratives: the frame with the speaker in the woods and then the inner story about the argument with the wife that led to her accident. How did you go about fusing these two pieces? Were they always in the same poem? Do you consider one or the other the more important story?

SL: From the start, they were one and the same story, the understandably complex tale of the moment(s) I recalled. There was no narrative engineering involved. My wife was near death; I was on a hike with two others who were close to her; I was at the very awkward and daunting dawn of what would be a long professorial career; a blind deer showed up; I felt—what I felt. I just tried to get all that onto the page as straightforwardly as I could, trusting that honest recollection would have its own poetry. I always operate on that trust, in fact.

DL: Chekhov said, *If you want to move your reader, write more coldly.* I couldn't help thinking of those words as I read and reread your poem. The tone is so chilly, but the poem is all the more effective because of that chilliness. How did you manage to keep out emotionalism and just let the details and images do their work?

SL: Well, I have always assumed that gushy sentimentality gets in the way of real sentiment. Once again, straightforward—even cold—recitation would carry the emotional freight I needed to make the poem other than a whine.

DL: There's irony in that the speaker who makes his living reading books and talking becomes *mute*, then *speechless*, and asks at the end, *What could I say?* He learns that there are *unspeakable things*. It's also ironic that the professor gets schooled by the logger. Did the irony come into the poem inadvertently or was it crafted?

SL: What I have always admired in the Yankee old-timer is his or her capacity to know the difference between acceptance and resignation. The old-timer I refer to (and I have lost touch with his son, a sort of bridge figure between his dad's emotional makeup and my own) is gone now; but as he once said, *If you can't fix something, you get along with it*. He had had a far more dangerous and at times tragic life than mine, and I am sure, as he was a very bright guy, he often wanted to say something about the unsayable; but because it was just that, he kept his counsel. I have never attained that height of philosophic thinking, but his is the sort of model I imagine when I find myself, or find another writer, too lavishly singing the aria in the opera called *MeMeMe*.

DL: I sense the ghost of Robert Frost in this poem. And although you do not name the setting, it feels like New England. What role, if any, have Frost and New England played in this poem?

SL: Yes, virtually all my poems are set in my home territory, New England north of Boston. There is no time spent in these villages and fields and woods that does not cause one, if he or she is a poet, and no matter what his or her taste and practices may be, to bring Frost to mind. Frost is not, maybe, my favorite poet, but he is surely the most influential on me. Harold Bloom would imagine some *anxiety of influence*, then, on my part; but I feel, rather, real gratitude to this mentor. He has opened my eyes to things that my own (comparatively) weak eyes wouldn't have caught.

Bonus Prompt: The Marriage of Heaven and Hell Poem

Remember an exquisitely happy experience. Freewrite about it for 5-10 minutes.

Now remember an exquisitely unhappy experience. Freewrite about it for 5-10 minutes.

For one of those experiences, the one that feels dominant, write a list of every detail of the setting that you can remember.

Begin your draft with the dominant experience. Include some of the setting details.

Interrupt with the other experience.

Return to and finish with the dominant one. Include some more of the setting details.

VII. Transformation

Poetry is a good provider of the strange.

—Dean Young

Craft Tip #19: Transformation by Ruination

—Ron Smith

Assuming you have an idea for a poem—perhaps a conversation to record or a landscape to describe—start your draft as rhyming quatrains in iambic meter or as an Italian sonnet, a villanelle, heroic couplets, or some other traditional form. Don't be critical, just fill out the form, jam the words in. Enjoy writing badly and serving frivolously the requirements of the form.

In revision, deploy those rules of good writing that you know: omit needless words, find a stronger verb (or no verb at all), remove the forced rhymes and the words that pad out the meter. What do you have now? A ruin, a bombed-out relic of traditional form.

Then ruin it some more. Ignoring your original form altogether, break your lines more effectively. Remember that the most meaningful and strongest position in the verse line is the end. Create syntactic ambiguity by placing the right word out there as a lighthouse or by hanging the right word out to dry. Consider the line as a meaningful unit, a unit that cuts across the meaning of the sentence.

Read your draft out loud, preferably to another person or into a voice recorder. What do you hear that you didn't notice before? Kill the bad, enhance the good.

Finally (if you're lucky), consider the shape of the overall poem on the page. Does the visual shape suggest or complement the meaning, the sound? Maybe it should. Does the poem look neat, orderly? Should it? Does the poem look ragged? What does the visual shape suggest about the heart and soul of the piece?

Now tinker—probably for weeks, maybe for years or decades. Read your draft when you're fresh and when you're exhausted. Read it in the morning, the afternoon, the evening. Read it when you're in a great mood; read it when you're in a terrible mood.

These encounters, these layers of response will help you see what you've done. Consider contractions, pronouns, punctuation.

It is said that Robert Frost put *finished* poems away for a year before he went back to them and declared them done. I'd say shorten that time—but make it long enough to forget what you had in mind in the early drafts. You can then read with objectivity, with aesthetic distance. Remember that you have to be, as Walt Whitman said, both in and out of the game. Become your Ideal Reader. Ask: What does it do to me? Does it *work*?

And what do you have? A ruined ruin? If you're fortunate, you won't end up with, say, a doubly dilapidated Parthenon haunted by tourist ghosts, but something more like the Sydney Opera House, alive with performances of the spirit.

However, if it *doesn't* work, try this (not for the faint of heart): Write a parody of your poem. Ask: What would my worst enemy say about this poem? What would he/she mock? Try to enjoy ridiculing your diction, your tone, your line breaks, your oh so precious sound effects.

Put it all away (of course, save *all* your drafts).

After a while, you can return to your parody. Lay a printed version of the parody next to your earlier draft, and contemplate what you've got. Every time I've done this, some of the parody has gotten incorporated into the actual poem.

Frost said, *No surprise for the writer, no surprise for the reader.* I would say, No pleasure for the writer, no pleasure for the reader. Find a way to enjoy the process. Even heart-rending elegies should be, weirdly, paradoxically, a delight to produce.

Poem and Prompt

Mercy

My chest's a knothole and my arm's a stick.
I creak and sigh like something on a hill.
No—that's my right side, left is human still—
So—I'm half tree, half me; half well, half sick.

What was it Daphne did? Did I do half?
It wasn't love I ran from—yet the birds
I watch approach me almost seem to laugh
as if they knew the lies I've told, the words

I always thought I meant. Ah—the human
side keeps digging, searching for a curse,
or something in the life, the shadow looming
in a thousand craven acts. "Have mercy,"

says the tree, as if it knew this hill
is not a judgment but a place to rest;
as if two mismatched halves could make me whole,
and sun and rain and earth could make me blessed.

—Hilde Weisert

We immediately notice the poem's leap of imagination as the speaker undergoes a transformation from woman to half woman and half tree. Line 4 leads us to understand that this transformation occurred during a period of illness.

In stanza 2 the speaker makes an allusion to mythological Daphne, a nymph who was changed into a laurel tree as she fled the advances of Apollo. The value of an allusion is that the poet with just a few words can bring in all the ideas associated with the original story. Notice the poet's use of questions to suggest the speaker's bewilderment. This is underscored by the use of dashes—five of them. They suggest the speed at which the speaker's mind is moving and, at the same time, force us to pause in our reading.

In the third stanza the tree is personified. While the woman becomes part tree, the tree becomes part human. In an unexpected turn at the end of the poem, the speaker reaches a resolution as her two halves merge and she feels *blessed*.

In spite of the oddness of the subject matter, Weisert uses a strict form for the poem—four rhymed quatrains. Stanza 1 is abba while the remaining three stanzas are abab. The poet uses perfect rhymes, e.g., *hill* and *still*, *stick* and *sick*. But she also uses near rhymes, e.g., *human* and *looming*, *curse* and *mercy*. Notice the use of iambic pentameter throughout.

For your own poem, think first of the kind of transformation that might occur in your poem and the reason for such a change. What kind of experience might make you feel as if you were only half the person you used to be? Perhaps illness, surgery, falling in or out of love, a divorce, the death of a loved one, moving to a new location. What might your other half become? Bird, fish, cat, rock, pickle?

Begin by freewriting for 10-20 minutes.

Consider bringing in an allusion, perhaps a mythological, biblical, or literary one. Choose one that somehow connects to your material.

Then work on the structure of the poem. Try a strict form for this poem and employ rhyme. Bonus points for meter.

Sample Poems

Alborado: Noun—Morning Song

I drink the Drink Me drink,
become more than night
person. Four lungs sing twice
notes, breathe deep, two times
magic. Blood flows new

through stented arteries.
Yeast rises early, doubles me.
I stand cheerfully at 5:30.
Face not aching, I don't hurry
to kill the kitchen radio.

I regift the mugs mocking
my desperate link to caffeine.
Morning, my secret found twin
now, we walk early in riverine
parks, like Writers of Books do.

Finally I can tell photos
of sunrises from sunsets.
Morning, you give minutes
to meditate in, sonnets,
yoga, time to garden, too.

I see angels, born new each
morning, I sing a baby tune,
"Is it good morning time?"
By calling out its own name,
the rising sun creates itself.

—Tina Kelley

Now That Your Gods Are Gone

The subject undoubtedly owed its sixteenth-century
popularity to the paradox that it was considered
more acceptable to depict a woman in the act of
copulation with a swan than with a man.
—Wikipedia

Barely ten you witnessed them once in a dark
motel room, you on your cot, your mother's
whispered no's and don'ts, his warbled pleas
in their overnight nest. Easier to fathom him
more bird than man, you story-booked his
imperious landing, feigned sleep, tried not
to overhear his advances forcing her,
innocent in the ways of stepfather gods.
As for your real father, you only saw her
touch him once, her hand on his balding head.

Old enough now yourself that both of your
gods are gone, passed away as mortals will,
you're half the daughter you used to be
times two, lighting candles for each man
on his *yahrzeit*, drawn to the traditional
annual flame. Sharing equally in their lives
and deaths, doubled in your father grief,
twice undone, you blink your kind
blue eyes from her first husband, at your
animal arrogance from the second. Split

down the middle of an awkward family tree,
you could be a Jewish Clytemnestra hatched
from Greek eggs. You could be Leda's daughter
spying within, hours after your own conception
from Tyndareus, at your mother as Zeus in his
vertical flutter-pose presses against her naked
recline. Impossible to untangle twisted damsel
from dropped deity as the swan locks between
Leda's hips, drapes his celestial wings under and
over her legs like a tufted cape, pins his beak to her
serene lips, her right arm curved around his coiled
white neck as if her surrender and smile hold him

to her, erotic, beautiful, satisfied until we remember
it's rape. Remember your mother's confession, how
before you were born she'd leave the ocean house
after your father had fallen asleep? Did her then-lover
down the beach leap out from the dunes in exquisite
disguise to seize her? Her men are your paradox,
your myths and your truths. Choosing sides gets
the better of you. But oh, how the grafted branches
amaze like this Baroque couple copied after
a lost Michelangelo. They hover post-coital over
puddled red silk Rubens chose for the background
to keep his seduction scene afloat while you swim
a private and public pool reflecting birds, love, blood.

—Kate Sontag

Craft Tip #20: Brush Up Those Formal Tools

—Meg Kearney

A few years ago, I was working on a poem I'd titled "Tattoo." It began as a three-page narrative poem that included not only how I got my tattoo and with whom, but also the tattoo artist's name (Rusty Savage—too good to leave out, right?). I thought I was onto something, but knew the poem needed help. Over the course of several weeks, I cut it to two pages, then to one; compression is the key to a poem's power, and these revisions definitely helped. Finally, I sent the one-page version to a trusted reader, who said, *When this poem is finished, it's going to be really good.* Her way of saying, *Back to your desk!*

I put the poem on the proverbial back burner and worked on other things. Still, the poem kept simmering in my mind. One of the best classes I took in graduate school was Prosody, taught by the late William Matthews. Bill's approach included asking his students to write a poem in a different form every week. He assured us that he didn't expect us to write a good sonnet or sestina or pantoum; he only wanted to see that we knew how each form worked, how it was made. If we followed the form correctly, he'd put a check at the top of the paper. Knowing we didn't have to be brilliant took all pressure off—we could truly investigate how those tools in our toolboxes worked, so that when we needed them, we'd know what to do.

While "Tattoo" was on that back burner, I started mentally going through the tools at my disposal. Then it hit me: the tattoo I was writing about was circular in form, like a pantoum. Why not try the poem in that form? Bingo. Poor Rusty came out, as did the whole story of how and why I'd gotten the tattoo. What was left was the surprise poem that had something to teach me, that revealed more than I knew that I knew.

These days I urge all poets, not just students, to consider writing in form more regularly. Form is very freeing, especially when tackling difficult emotional subjects, as focus on the structure of the poem tends to shut up that internal editor who says, *You can't write that* or *What a horrible line!* Form enables the imagination to make leaps and associations it would not otherwise make.

Give it a shot—you just might surprise yourself. You just might write your best poem yet.

Poem and Prompt

Stillbirth

On a platform, I heard someone call out your name:
No, Laetitia, no.
It wasn't my train—the doors were closing,
but I rushed in, searching for your face.

But no Laetitia. No.
No one in that car could have been you,
but I rushed in, searching for your face:
no longer an infant. A woman now, blond, thirty-two.

No one in that car could have been you.
Laetitia-Marie was the name I had chosen.
No longer an infant. A woman now, blond, thirty-two:
I sometimes go months without remembering you.

Laetitia-Marie was the name I had chosen:
I was told not to look. Not to get attached—
I sometimes go months without remembering you.
Some griefs bless us that way, not asking much space.

I was told not to look. Not to get attached.
It wasn't my train—the doors were closing.
Some griefs bless us that way, not asking much space.
On a platform, I heard someone calling your name.

—Laure-Ann Bosselaar

This form is called a *pantoum*. Let's try one. But first its rules.

1. A pantoum consists of a series of quatrains. There is no set number.

2. The second and fourth lines of each stanza are repeated as the first and third lines of the next stanza. This pattern continues for any number of stanzas, except for the final stanza.

3. The first and third lines of the final stanza are the second and fourth lines of the second to last stanza. The second line of the final stanza is the third line of the first stanza and the fourth line of the final stanza is the first line of the first stanza.

4. Ideally, the meaning of lines shifts when they are repeated even though the words remain the same. Meaning can be altered by context and punctuation. Also, this rule can be broken a bit. You might want to vary the wording somewhat in the repeating lines.

5. Line lengths may vary.

6. Now do not have a heart attack, but there's also supposed to be a rhyme pattern of abab in each stanza. However, once you get beyond the first stanza, that will just fall into place. And here's the good news: you are free to abandon rhyming. Notice that Bosselaar does not follow the prescribed rhyming pattern, though she does employ some rhyme.

The pantoum says everything twice. That makes it an ideal form for obsessive subjects. Notice how Bosselaar's repetitions hammer away at you, how effectively they convey grief. The loss of a child lasts forever. The sorrow keeps coming back.

As you approach your own pantoum, you may find it helpful, even essential, to write the pattern down the right or left side of your page before you begin writing the poem. For example, a

4-quatrain pantoum with rhyme would have the following pattern. Numbers are for the lines; letters are for the rhyme scheme:

1 a
2 b
3 a
4 b

2 b
5 c
4 b
6 c

5 c
7 d
6 c
8 d

7 d
3 a
8 d
1 a

Think of something that repeatedly returns to your mind, perhaps an experience that haunts you. The spouse who did you wrong. The missed opportunity that seems to have altered the course of your life. The heirloom you lost. The forgiveness you failed to give or receive. Treatment for a long illness. Giving birth.

While the form lends itself nicely to heavy topics, it also works well with lighter subjects. For example, are you obsessing about chocolate? About getting your weight down? About this year's marathon?

Don't be intimidated by the form. Once you get going, you'll see that it falls into place. Some of you will labor over your lines; others of you will find that the poem pours right out of you. Keep coming back to it until you have a satisfactory draft. Then work on it until it's a gem.

Sample Poems

For Kristie

The night is cold and lit by moonlight.
Her room is quiet, a soft light glows.
Voices whisper—there is no answer.
The bed sheets rustle, the tumor grows.

Her room is quiet, a soft light glows.
Upon her back we place our hands.
The bed sheets rustle, the tumor grows
and we attempt to soothe her pain.

Upon her back we place our hands.
The morphine drips into her veins
and we attempt to soothe her pain.
While her body twists and turns,

the morphine drips into her veins.
Voices whisper, "There is no answer."
While her body twists and turns,
the night is cold and lit by moonlight.

—Kim Klugh

The Abundance of Budding

This is what I know, this is the truth:
I forgot about the flowering,
the moon-wide face of magnolias
outside our upstairs window.

I forgot about the flowering,
the thrum of words aroused in distant rain
outside our upstairs window
to glimpse a fevered ache of blue.

The thrum of words aroused in distant rain
a musky citrus scent of creamy blooms.
The sky sharpened into certainty blue,
raindrops balanced on every leaf.

The musky citrus scent of creamy blooms
blended with lavender bounding along the fence.
Raindrops quivered on every petal,
contentment palpable in the monsoon-wet air.

Remember how lavender bounded wild along
the fence beneath the moon-wide face of magnolias?
How enchantment shimmered in the steamy air?
This is the truth, this is what I know.

—Kathy Macdonald

Craft Tip #21: New Eyes

—Laura Kasischke

The best poems are the ones that bring the familiar world to us, and then reveal it to us in strange new ways. It's this experience of having our eyes opened, our perspective changed, that draws us to reading poetry, but I would propose that it is also a way of approaching the writing of poetry—the search for new eyes with which to regard a place, a person, or an experience—that can move the poems we might write from good to great. It is a mental trick that can be practiced any time, or all the time, and then brought to the process of poetry writing. It could be called, simply, *defamiliarization.*

In an anecdote from his book *The Night Sky,* the anthropologist Richard Grossinger writes of an experience he had while attending a meeting of people who believed they had been abducted by aliens. In my opinion, it is a spontaneous experience with defamiliarization:

> At a UFO meeting that I attended in the basement of a bank in Hamtramck, Michigan, the gathering was told that it was honored by visitors from Venus and Saturn. I looked around the room, and suddenly everyone appeared strange and extraterrestrial. Everyone was a candidate.

Such experiences are not rare—that feeling that occurs occasionally while, say, standing in line at the bank, when for a second the mental curtain is lifted and you see how strange this is, all these two-eyed creatures with coiffed dead cells sprouting from their heads, holding pieces of paper they will eventually exchange for food or lipsticks.

When a poet practices the intentional act of peering under that curtain, the result can be a great poem. Defamiliarization takes the subject matter of a piece of writing out of the ordinary prose world and into the world of poetry.

How is this defamiliarization accomplished?

First, one needs to be conscious of it as a goal. Then, during the writing process, in order to defamiliarize oneself with one's subject matter, one needs be rid of the baggage—the intellectual and emotional associations that are firmly attached to the subject. One needs to be able to find a path by which to return to the *original* features of the thing, not so much to *see it new*, though that's important, but to *see it naked*. And to put the nakedness on the page.

Contrast is the quickest route to defamiliarization. Contrast is, of course, why metaphor itself is the most important tool of poetry—because a new understanding of a subject, object, or experience is brought to it by contrast.

When your mother in her house slippers is moved, in a poem, from your 1950's living room to Mars, there is a whole new way of considering her slippers. If she is shape-shifted in your poem from the Suzanne Sullivan you knew so well into a dolphin wearing her house slippers, you have a whole new way to consider her experience, your love for her, her hopes, despair, and feet. Before you sit down to write about your mother packing you a lunch to take to school, you may ask yourself what kind of lunch your mother would have packed for you to take to school had you never been born.

This is defamiliarization through contrast. The mental exercises that can shift our understanding and bring us to real insights are endless. This is a part of the poetry-writing process that will become completely natural to you after you have met with success (which is surprise) with it in a few poems that opened up your new eyes.

Poem and Prompt

Sincerely, the Sky

Yes, I see you down there
looking up into my vastness.

What are you hoping
to find on my vacant face,

there between the crisscross
of telephone wires?

You should know I am only
bright blue now because of physics:

molecules break and scatter
my light from the sun

more than any other color.
You know my variations—

azure at noon, navy by midnight.
How often I find you

then on your patio, pajamaed
and distressed, head thrown

back so your eyes can pick apart
not the darker version of myself

but the carousel of stars.
To you I am merely background.

You barely hear my voice.
Remember I am most vibrant

when air breaks my light.
Do something with your brokenness.

—David Hernandez

In this epistolary poem, that is, one that poses as a letter, Hernandez pulls off a few surprises. First, the title is the letter's closing and signature, so the poem begins with its ending.

Then Hernandez uses direct address as his speaker, the sky, speaks to a human below. The poet also uses personification as he gives the sky both a voice and a face.

Notice how the question in stanzas 2-3 prepares for what immediately follows: a scientific fact brought in from the field of physics. This fact gets some elaboration in the next three stanzas. We then realize that the human is sleepless and seems distressed, though we don't know why. Hernandez closes the poem with a stunning imperative. This comes as a complete surprise, yet is well prepared for in stanza 5's *molecules break* and the penultimate line's *when air breaks my light*.

The diction is this poem is simple and effective. Notice, particularly, the preposition used in the last line: *Do something with your brokenness*. How would the poem change if the poet had said *about* instead of *with*? Small as they are, prepositions matter.

For your epistolary poem, first choose what you would like to use as the speaker, e.g., the ocean, a stone, thunder, grass, a salmon. Do a bit of research and find a few obscure but intriguing facts about your speaker.

Now title your draft with your letter's closing. You might use *Yours truly, Love, Best, Take care, Thanks,* or *With affection.* Add a comma and your signature.

Freewrite for about 20 minutes. Remembering that this is a letter, use first person point of view. Try to inhabit the body of your speaker, i.e., become the grass or the salmon. Use direct address and keep imagining that you are speaking to a human. That human might or might not be someone you know.

What question would you like to ask your person? Put that in the poem.

Insert your fact and some details into the draft. Provide a clue or two that your human is troubled, or perhaps joyful.

Aim for a stunning last line, one that somehow connects to the scientific fact. It should come as a surprise to you.

Keep your diction simple for this poem. Pay attention to your prepositions.

Sample Poems

Forever yours, the Coachella Desert

Remember your barefoot years when you loved
my arid air?
You return now to view the ruins
of my barrios, a contrast to

the casinos, golf courses, and gated
communities encroaching on my aching back,

my Salton Sea, once lovely,
now infested with waste
from farms and pumped-in toxins,

abuzz with swarms of flies. No more
the dusty, date-palm arms you knew.

No matter how you resist me, I will always be your first
lover. My fiery kiss forever branded on your brown skin.

—Anjela Villarreal Ratliff

Sincerely, the Mulberry

I know I would've been hauled
away with the wire fence and ivy
if the gardener hadn't voted I stay—
for the birds. That was fall
and now I stand ready to bud.
All winter I waited but you
never looked. You'd reach one arm out,
drop junk mail into the recycling bin,
your feet still planted inside.
Nights, through the curtainless window,
I watch you stand at the sink,
not washing the dishes.
Lamp by lamp the house goes dark.
Even at the back door's long panes,
it seems you are not looking out
but in, as if you saw something inside
through the backs of your eyes.
The pregnant cats know your back porch
as the warmest place on the block.
Afternoons, they rest heavy bellies
in quadrangles of light.
Orange crocuses bloom then shrivel.
Deer graze as if no one lived here.
Mornings, Mae walks the alley,
one hand on her cane, the other
holding her granddaughter's hand—
they too see what you miss.
You should know: I'm not a weed anymore.
Decisions were made. I have a shape now.
Soon I'll have a round shadow.
Don't miss my bloom.

—Lori Wilson

The Poet on the Poem: Alice Friman

Coming Down

At high altitudes the heart rises
to throat level, clanging for service.
The body—#1 customer—needs oxygen,
the red blood cells scurrying like beaten
serfs not delivering fast enough: supply
and demand, that old saw.
                            Remember
struggling to make love under six blankets,
my heart banging so hard it threatened
to knock me out of bed, and you
in socks, ski hat, and four sweaters, fighting
for breath? When relating our story, paring
it down for parties,
                        let's leave those parts
out. Say we went to South America
for pre-Columbian art and Machu Picchu.
Mention the giant condors, yes, but not how
they floated up from Colca Canyon
like human souls circling in great flakes
of praise
            nor how I cried, reaching to bridge
the unbridgeable gap. Say that one shivering
night we visited a thermal pool, but not
how slippery as twins tumbling in the womb,
we sloshed together under Andean stars.
Or how nose-bleeding or heart-pounding
and laboring for breath,
                            always always
we reached for each other. Practice the lesson
of the body in distress: the heart knows
how much leeway it has before demanding
its due. Waiting in line for the Xerox calls for
giveaways of more supple truths: cartilage, Love,
not bone.

DL: What was the thinking behind your decision to use dropped lines? What do you think they contribute to the poem?

AF: The poem is in the form of a sort of letter—a mental letter to my husband. But, yes, a letter; therefore, the paragraph form with what I think of as paragraph indentations rather than dropped lines. I think that the paragraph form is useful when a stanza break seems like too much of a break and the alternative is no break at all. It's a sort of compromise, a middle ground, a little break.

When I write, I rarely think about how the poem presents itself on the page. The underlying emotional heart of a given piece usually chooses how it wants to come out. In a first draft, scribbled in ink, the line breaks and stanza breaks will often naturally assert themselves. And then later, after many drafts, I back up and take a look. In the case of this piece, the first two stanzas came out in six lines each. All right, I say, six-line stanzas is what you want? So be it.

DL: The poem includes several negatives: in stanza 3 *but not*, in stanza 4 *nor how* and another *but not*, and in the poem's last line *not bone*. There's also a contrast between what really happened and what the two lovers will say happened. And there's a contrast between what the physical heart wants and what the romantic heart wants. Talk to us about the function and value of contrast in this poem.

AF: Yes, there's much contrast in the poem, and I'm pleased that you pointed it out. But use of contrast is only one part of a process of clarification and narrowing down that this poem employs. The poem begins with the general and little by little moves to the particular. In this case: bone. More important to that process of narrowing is that the piece is written in the negative. Writing in the negative is a technique I use often. What it does is clarify by paring down in steps: no it's not this, nor is it this, nor this, until you get to the point, the conclusion.

I hasten to say that I think if a poet chooses to employ the negative, it's not necessary to have thought about the end before sitting down to write the poem. That's an essay, not a poem.

Robert Frost said that a poem is an ice cube melting on the stove. In other words, the poem should be a discovery for the writer in writing it as it is for the reader in absorbing it.

I think writing a poem utilizing a repetition of the negative serves as an example of the poet thinking on paper. And hopefully, the reader, in following the negative steps, becomes a companion to that thinking, thus leading him down, down to the point—in the case of this particular poem, to *cartilage, Love, / not bone*. Notice, too, that the poem begins with the body and ends with the body, and so, in a sense, the poem is a circular descending spiral driven by all those negatives.

DL: The repetition of *always* in the final indented line strikes me as one of those little things that mean a lot. Is it strategic? Why repeat the word?

AF: Yes, it's strategic. I repeat the word for emphasis. After all, the poem is a love poem. Even under great physical duress (which we were in) and in the midst of incredible beauty that bordered on the mythic, making us feel small and insignificant, we clung to each other. Yes we did. That is the *bone* I'm referring to at the end, the basic bone of our marriage that isn't necessary to share with idle chat at the water cooler. There's an old Irving Berlin song called "Always" that my husband often sings to me in his sweet tenor voice, a song that always makes me cry. In it the word *always* is repeated and repeated. Perhaps I was channeling that.

DL: Your poem is rich with figurative language. For example, hyperbole occurs in stanza 2 where you have a *heart banging so hard it threatened / to knock me out of bed* and in stanza 4 where the two lovers were *nose-bleeding or heart-pounding / and laboring for breath*. Hyperbole often doesn't work in serious poems, but it does in yours. Tell us how you made it work.

AF: My dictionary defines hyperbole as *an obvious and intentional exaggeration*. Let me assure you that the language I use is neither exaggeration nor hyperbole. We were in the mountains of Peru. We were over 16,000 feet up. I did some research after I got home to understand just how high we were so as to explain the effect that that altitude had on us, especially me. Denver is called *the mile high city*. Its altitude is only 5,183 feet—one third as high as where we were. Sixteen thousand feet is higher than any mountain in the Alps. Twenty-six thousand feet is called *the death zone*. I can tell you honestly and plainly that I understand why. When I speak of *nose-bleeding* in the poem, I am recalling the fact that I ended up in the emergency room gushing from both nostrils. When I say *heart-pounding*, I can tell you that when the heart is laboring so hard, the rest of your body feels like an appendage to be knocked about. If you are lying down, the body twitches uncontrollably and jerks back and forth hard. I did indeed feel as if I were going to be knocked out of bed.

DL: You employ several similes. In stanza 1 we find *red blood cells scurrying like beaten / serfs*, in stanza 3 condors *floated... / like human souls*, and in stanza 4 we are told that the lovers were once *slippery as twins tumbling in the womb*. Are these similes to be taken as literally as your hyperboles? How did you arrive at these comparisons?

AF: When I wrote *the red blood cells scurrying like beaten / serfs*, I was thinking that red blood cells carry oxygen. People who live in the higher elevations of the Andes have evolved larger red blood cells that are capable of delivering more oxygen. We, on the other hand, are at a disadvantage; the heart has to pump like crazy to drive the blood faster and faster. I imagined the red blood cells as serfs, bent under their load of oxygen, being whipped and driven.

One of the most magical places I've ever seen is Colca Canyon which is twice as deep as the Grand Canyon. You sit on the edge and watch the condors with wingspans of up to ten and a half feet float slowly up out of the canyon. Since they are so big, they have to wait until the sun warms the air enough so that they can rise on the thermals. They do not *fly* as we know it but float instead, being lifted up and then circling. They seemed weightless like great dark flakes. Before I left, I stood, tilted back my head, and raised my arms; one condor seemed to pause, then circle above me like some sort of greeting, and I felt as if I were being blessed. The fact that most people were fussing with their cameras and two men standing next to me were discussing their golf game made me realize again how perhaps I don't belong in this world, which is why I listed this experience as one of the things *not* to be discussed in passing, in idle chat.

The *tumbling in the womb* refers to one very cold night high in the Andes when we visited a thermal pool. The water was hot as amniotic fluid, the earth's uterine water, and my beloved and I were playing in it. Were we not then children of the earth? twins in the belly of the mother? in the world's amniotic sack?

As for how I arrived at these similes, I just wrote what I saw and what it meant to me.

DL: It's clear that your poem evolved out of a real experience. What made you sit down and convert the experience into a poem?

AF: Not all poems have a trigger, that is, the thing that gets you started—but this one did, an interesting one. My husband and I had recently come back from Peru, so, of course, our stay there was in my mind and I had been writing about it. It was a late afternoon. I was driving on the outskirts of Columbus, Georgia, I imagine coming home from the Carson McCullers house where I used to go to hole up and write. I passed a street sign that said—or I thought it said—*Cartilage Drive*. That caught me up. Wow! Cartilage? And I realized that I had never seen that word in a poem. Okay, I said. I shall write a poem whose end will include the word *cartilage*.

Bonus Prompt: The Repurposed Haiku

This is a wonderful warm-up activity, perfect for those times when you're convinced that you have no poems left in you. The activity is quick and easy and has the added bonus of often leading to a keeper poem.

Find a book of haiku poems. If you don't have any handy, do a Google search. Gather together a bunch of haiku poems.

Choose one haiku that has words you like.

Write each word, one per line, down the left side of a piece of paper.

Each word begins a new line of your new poem. If your borrowed haiku has ten words, your poem will have ten lines. If your borrowed haiku has twelve words, then your poem will have twelve lines.

Now write your poem.

Remember: You are not writing a haiku poem.

VIII. Special Forms

Poetry: three mismatched shoes at the entrance of a dark alley.

—Charles Simic

Craft Tip #22: The Mask Behind the Mask: The Dramatic Monologue

—Lee Ann Roripaugh

Dramatic monologues, also known as persona poems, draw freely in their craft and technique from the genres of playwriting, fiction, and poetry, making them, to my mind, a hybrid-genre form rich with exciting cross-genre possibilities.

Paradoxically, the dramatic monologue emerges from a tricky welding together of the completely disparate elements of artifice and authenticity. Constructing a first-person character or persona who speaks from the page and engages the reader's imagination in such a way that disbelief is willingly suspended is, in many respects, a tour-de-force of creative artifice. It relies upon creating a compelling and nuanced character that seemingly speaks naturally and authentically from a believable scene/setting/narrative circumstance—all of which are artificial illusions created by and through language and voice. Yet when these elements successfully come together, the dramatic monologue is a powerfully resonant form—one that uncannily captures the interior psychological landscape of a character/speaker.

In many respects, the dramatic monologist dons the linguistic and psychological mask of the speaker much in the way that a skilled actor prepares for an acting role. Think about Daniel Day Lewis in *My Left Foot*, being wheel-barrowed about the set throughout the duration of filming, refusing to use any of his limbs other than his left foot. Or think of Canadian actress Tatiana Maslany in the BBC's *Orphan Black* chameleon-ing her way through the multiple, diversely distinct characters of the *clone club*—occasionally even engaging in virtuoso acting stunts in which she believably plays one clone impersonating another clone.

The dramatic monologue relies upon the fiction writer's keen sense of characterization, as well as the dramaturge's flair for framing narrative tension—creating a dramatic moment that not only reveals the nature of the character speaking, but also provides the narrative scaffolding around which the character speaks, and which may even prompt the character to speak.

The dramatic monologue is an intimate form. It reveals the interior life of the character, as held in tension with the exterior, public mask. Thus, it is a layering of masks: the writer donning the mask of the speaker of the dramatic monologue, who—as all people do—wears one or more public masks. There is an element of voyeurism in reading or hearing a dramatic monologue—the sense of eavesdropping or spying upon the character, or secretly reading someone's personal email. It is a private expression, paradoxically made manifest within the public sphere of the page or the stage. Strangely, dramatic monologues sometimes become profoundly confessional poems for poets who, behind the protective scrim of the mask, may find themselves revealing something excruciatingly personal about themselves.

Like the novelist, or the method actor, the dramatic monologist must learn everything there is to know about the chosen character, even though only ten percent, at most, will likely appear within the frame of the poem. Speaking from this deep reservoir of details, however, allows the dramatic monologist to understand their character, and to easily and naturally pull from these details on an as-needed basis, as well as understand the psychological underpinnings about what makes the character perceive, act, respond, obsess, fear, dream, and desire in a particular way. The dramatic monologue is a poetic form that frequently benefits from intense research. In my experience of writing dramatic monologues, when I've researched and processed enough information and details about my characters, I find that their voices simply start coming to me, one by one—like tapping into a wi-fi signal.

The craft elements of voice and tone are crucial to creating the linguistic and psychological mask of a dramatic monologue. Voice involves the diction of a particular speaker or character: the word choice, vocabulary, dialect, slang, and colloquialisms. Tone, however, is the character's attitude and/or emotional climate, which is fluid, and can shift during the course of a monologue. Tone is subtle, and draws upon the fiction writer's toolkit of narrative reliability and dialogic subtext. Tone is the magic by which the character might unconsciously reveal something significant about himself to the readers—not through the actual words of what he is saying, but how he says it (or doesn't say it) through the tonal undercurrents.

For me, the monologue has been a particularly powerful form that I've found useful for poems of social activism: poems which privilege the recuperation of potentially silenced voices in lieu of linguistic dexterity or poetic image-making. Drawing upon my Japanese heritage, I've written monologues in the fictional voices of Japanese-American internees relocated to Heart Mountain Relocation Camp in Wyoming during World War II, a Hiroshima Maiden, and fictional survivors of Fukushima, for example.

But there is, I feel, an ethics to dramatic monologue writing, much as there is an ethics to documentary photography, and I believe the dramatic monologist needs to be particularly careful not to engage in inappropriate (even if well-meaning) acts of cultural appropriation and/or ventriloquism of marginalized voices. How does one know if a story is one's to tell? I don't have easy answers for this, even with respect to my own work. I do know that respectful engagement is key, along with scrupulous research, as well as listening for a very long time before allowing your characters to enter the page and begin speaking.

Poem and Prompt

Self-Portrait as Mae West One-Liner

I'm no moaning bluet, mountable
linnet, mumbling nun. I'm
tangible, I'm gin. Able to molt
in toto, to limn. I'm blame and angle, I'm
lumbago, an oblate mug gone notable,
not glum. I'm a tabu tuba mogul, I'm motile,
I'm nimble. No gab ennui, no bagel bun-boat: I'm one
big mega-ton bolt able to bail
men out. Gluten iamb. Male bong unit.
I'm a genial bum, mental obi, genital
montage. I'm Agent Limbo, my blunt bio
an amulet, an enigma. Omit elan. Omit bingo.
Alien mangle, I'm glib lingo. Untangle me,
tangelo. But I'm no angel.

—Paisley Rekdal

Most readers of this poem will first notice its exuberant language. The poem is a feast of odd but musical words. Where do they come from? It might take a while for the reader to realize that this is a kind of form poem, one that relies on a game you probably played in school: the *anagram*. One of the pleasures of an anagram poem is the music it makes. Because you are using the same letters to form your words, you'll get lots of rhymes and near rhymes as well as assonance, consonance, and alliteration.

Mae West fans probably recognize the last line, *I'm no angel*, as the title of Mae West's third movie, filmed in 1933. To that line, Rekdal has added the word *But*.

Rekdal's anagram poem is also an oddball self-portrait and a strange persona poem. It doesn't make a lot of literal sense, but it makes a kind of sense. We get the feeling that Rekdal's speaker is a zany person, fanciful, bold, imperfect, and complicated.

For your own poem, first choose a memorable line. The line should not be too long, approximately fifteen letters, including a number of vowels. It should be a line that might be used to describe the speaker of your self-portrait. Your line might be a movie title (e.g., *The Terminator* or *Bride of Frankenstein*), a line from a movie (e.g., *like I'm a clown* or *I am in my prime*), a line from a song (e.g., *the gangster of love* or *doesn't mean I'm lonely*), or something a famous person said (e.g., *déjà vu all over again* or *I have not failed*).

Write your line on a piece of paper. Then create a list of words made from the letters in your line. Get as many as you can. Short words and long words. Nouns, verbs, adjectives. Don't worry about what you're going to do with them. One rule: no letter can be used more than once in the same word unless it appears more than once in your line.

Now you're ready to begin your poem. For the first draft, title your poem "Self-Portrait as _____," and fill in the blank.

Since this is a self-portrait poem, use the first person *I*. If your borrowed line doesn't contain the letter *i*, you can add it. Use your line in the poem, maybe at the beginning or the end.

Rekdal added two words, *and* and *but*, to her poem. You may allow yourself one or two add-ons for the sake of the poem. You might strive for the 14-line structure of Rekdal's poem, but let your words determine that.

In describing herself, the speaker in Rekdal's poem creates metaphor after metaphor, e.g., *she's gin, an oblate mug, Alien mangle*. Be sure you include some metaphors, too.

In revising your poem, consider changing the title and making the poem a biography by switching to third person.

Sample Poems

Self-Portrait Featuring Emily Dickinson's Best Pick-Up Line

Hey dynamo—
you bawdy moon! Bide your yawn.
I'm your hyena, moon byway, hum doorway,
body unwary.

I'm no rue body, no moody bayou,
no weary domino,
no wry boom audio.

I? Honey womb, hid omen,
yaw rebound,
body amen.

Oh now, you embryo id—
obey any drum
on rodeo whim!
Obey yum. Embody our woo:
a you/me hybrid...

So anyhow:
I'm nobody—who are you?

—Tracy Hart

Self-Portrait from a Warren Zevon One-Liner

I'm spawned in a hen pen, deal mead
as I please, wade hip deep in mean men.
I'm slain as slim sheep—plead—leap
pill piles. I whap a slip lip, wail a need
made new, slam dawn in plaid dew,
dip a pen in pine weeds, shed deeds, dim.

Planed a wall plaid, pawned a lawn,
mined a lead dime, aped a dame, peed
ale in a mall. Wed. Wine-head.
I'll sleep when I'm dead.

—Camille Norvaisas

Craft Tip #23: An Invitation to the Prose Poetry Party

—Nin Andrews

I have been writing prose poems for thirty years, and in the earlier years of my career, certain editors would not even consider publishing a prose poem. Now, although prose poetry has gained considerable acceptance, I still run across editors and poets who are suspicious of the form. I continue to be asked, *Why prose poems?* A question that is usually followed by the question: *How do you define prose poetry?* I want to answer that I don't, though Russell Edson's comparison of a prose poem to an airplane always comes to mind. *A prose poem,* Edson wrote, *is like a cast iron aeroplane that can fly, mainly because its pilot does not care if it does or not.*

I absolutely believe that prose poems can fly, or at least they can give me the sensation of lifting off, defying gravity, the very weight of form, logic, tradition, definitions. Sometimes I think that it is the wish to escape form and logic that inspires many prose poets. Many make a game of playing with these very definitions, and it is this game I would like to invite you to play. And I mean literally and literarily to play.

So much of the pleasure of prose poetry can be derived from its ability not only to incorporate but also to mock and/or mimic other forms of writing. Max Jacob, for example, wrote a prose poem, which resembled a tiny novella. Carol Maldow's novel, *The Widening*, is actually a series of prose poems. Russell Edson, Greg Boyd, and Julio Cortazar have written prose poems that are parables, myths, and fairy tales or perhaps anti-parables, anti-myths, and anti-fairy tales. Stacey Harwood wrote a prose poem based on contributors' notes. Robert Miltner has a prose poem that mimics a word problem. Amy Gerstler has one prose poem that looks like a page of singles ads, another which looks like a page from a name your baby book. And another, "Dear Boy George," which is a parody of a fan letter. In my *Book of Orgasms*, one poem is an interview with an orgasm, another an ad, and another a glossary of selected terms.

In *Supernatural Overtones*, the book of prose poems by Ron Padgett and Clark Coolidge, it appears that Coolidge wrote language poems, and Padgett interpreted them as if they were old sci-fi movies. Ron Padget's prose poem, "Falling in Love in Spain," is structured like a short play in which the main character's lines are borrowed from a Spanish-language phrase book. And I could go on. The possibilities seem limitless. So why not try one?

As I write this, I am thinking of ideas. Why not write a prose poem that is a recipe? I am reminded of Simic's line: *Margaret was copying a recipe for Saints Roasted with Onions from an old cookbook,* but what would the recipe be? What about a recipe for summer? For silence? For surviving tuna noodle casserole? Or maybe write a poem that is an obituary. An obituary for silence or tuna noodle casserole or summer or a love affair or poetry. Or a poem that is a chain letter. A poem that is a list of New Year's resolutions. A poem that is a personals ad. A poem that is a self-help column. A poem that is a love letter. A poem that is a horoscope, a grocery list, a table of contents, an invitation, a dictionary entry, an apology, a revelation, a confession to a priest.

Choose one and see what happens. Or choose two or three. Why not?

Whatever you choose, decide what is the most compelling aspect of the form. Just for the fun of it, you might decide to add food to every poem. (I have this theory that food is a nice addition to almost any poem.) If you are writing a self-help poem, for example, you might want to suck in your reader by creating a sense of intimacy with his or her suffering. Maybe begin with something like: *Are you, too, suffering from a loss of appetite? Lusterless lunches? Are your peaches bruised? Your eggs cold? Are there no noodles in your broth?*

If you are writing a poem that is a horoscope, maybe offer something exciting or a little threatening to your reader. *Your life will be upended on the 9th of July at precisely 3 PM. But don't let that hinder your ambitious nature or your appetite for bliss and pasta marinara.*

If you are writing a dictionary entry, you might mimic the form closely but let your imagination run free. For example, you could define a word like *lust*:

> Lust: noun 1. a fire that begins in the gut and travels to the fingers and toes 2. an unsung song 3. the last time you saw her sipping a Starbucks latté but could not bring yourself to say her name aloud.

Then you might want to add synonyms and antonyms and examples. This might become a prose poem about the unnamed girl. Or about a fire that began in the girl's fingers and took over the neighborhood. Or of the song sung by the fire and the girl that no one heard. (Okay, maybe this one would be better without the Starbucks latté.)

Of course, you can make any of these examples or games more personal by using the first person, free-associating, and including details of your own life, real or imagined. In other words, you could define a word like *grapefruit* and have a definition be something like:

> 1. the fruit my mother once said was imported from the moon. 2. the only food my first girlfriend, Cecelia Jones, would eat. She sat at the lunch table, strands of her long black hair falling across her face, spooning grapefruit between her pink lips.

But whatever you decide, have fun, play, go wild. As you can see, even thinking of the possibilities that prose poetry offers inspires me. Makes me happy. And makes me want to write. If nothing else, prose poetry is fun. It can be a springboard into the imagination, memory, magic. It is the one dance floor where all literary and not-so-literary forms can come together to meet, mingle, and share moves. Everyone is invited to the party.

Poem and Prompt

Soaking Up Sun

Today there is the kind of sunshine old men love, the kind of day when my grandfather would sit on the south side of the wooden corncrib where the sunlight warmed slowly all through the day like a woodstove. One after another dry leaves fell. No painful memories came. Everything was lit by a halo of light. The cornstalks glinted bright as pieces of glass. From the fields and grove came the rich smell of mushrooms, of things going back to earth. I sat with my grandfather then. Sheep came up to us as we sat there, their oily wool so warm to my fingers, a strange and magic snow. My grandfather whittled sweet smelling apple sticks just to get at the center. His thumb had a permanent groove in it where the back of the knife blade pressed. He let me listen to the wind, the wild geese, the soft dialect of sheep, while his own silence taught me every secret thing he knew.

—Tom Hennen

In this prose poem Tom Hennen gives us a scene with minimal action. The speaker, now a man, recalls how he used to sit with his grandfather by the corncrib. Leaves fell, sheep moved, the grandfather whittled sticks. The two listened but did not speak.

The speaker begins in the present time but quickly moves into the past, into memory. As that movement occurs, the poem unobtrusively switches from present to past tense.

Notice how subtly the grandfather is characterized—with little action and no words at all; instead, gestures and silence reveal the man. Notice especially the telling detail of the thumb, the *permanent groove in it where the back of the knife blade pressed.* That single detail reveals a man who worked hard with his hands.

Like any other kind of poem, a prose poem pays attention to the elements of poetry. This prose poem relies on imagery for its success. We have images of light. The sunshine was a *halo of light* and cornstalks *glinted*. We also have sound images: the wind, the geese, the sheep. Then there are olfactory images: the *rich smell of mushrooms* and the *sweet smelling apple sticks*. Finally, the sense of touch plays a role as the boy is warmed by the sun and the *oily wool* of the sheep.

All of these images create a feeling of warmth, of closeness to the earth and the things of the earth. This warmth and closeness become emblematic of the relationship between the boy and his grandfather.

Notice also the use of similes and metaphors in this prose poem: *the sunlight warmed slowly all through the day like a woodstove*, the *cornstalks glinted bright as pieces of glass*, and the sheep's oily wool was *a strange and magic snow*.

For your own poem, recall a person who mattered to you, who exerted influence and made some kind of impression on you. This may be but need not be someone you were close to.

Think of a single revealing action performed by the selected person.

Now put that person in a specific location. List several relevant details of your setting.

Choose a single day and a limited time period in that day or night.

Before you begin drafting, create some appropriate images:

　　1. List some images pertaining to light or darkness.

　　2. List some sound images.

　　3. List some smell images.

　　4. List some touch images.

Now you're ready to begin your first draft. Using first person point of view, begin with the present tense in the present time. Let something in the present time touch off the memory of the past. Switch to past tense.

Work in your images. Get in some similes and/or metaphors.

Try the prose poem format. Put your poem in a box.

Sample Poems

Language of First Light

The blue mist of dawn hangs over the mountains, the kind of morning Gram would shake me awake, nightfall still blowing under the door. In the kitchen, we pulled on boots and gloves as the wind carried the sound of anxious neighing. Through tendrils of fog, the smudged shapes of horses lined the paddock fence. We doled out their morning feed, suffused in their warm earthy smells, as they nuzzled the top of our heads. In the barn, Gram stood motionless and squinted up at the loft where daybreak illuminated a horde of dragonflies, hovering outside the window. *Flick, flick* against the glass. Their muffled wings beat a whole language of grief against the pane, trying to free a compatriot dragonfly trapped on the inside with us. With a broom, Gram climbed the loft stairs and extended the long handle to the dragonfly. It lighted on the end like a mounted specimen, large compound eyes facing her, wings stilled. Rung by rung, Gram lowered her feet to the ground, tiptoed across the barn, and stepped outside. The dragonfly surged up to the outer loft window. All was aflutter: the universe transformed into a squall of shimmery wings. Gram smiled at me, her dimples long since furrowed into sunbaked crevices. She always spoke to me with silence like a cloud or a tree. Or the stalwart gaze of a horse. In her stillness, she taught me the language of light on this lush blue planet.

—Kathy Macdonald

Daddy Comes Home from Angelo's Coney Island, Flint, Michigan

My sister reaches into her suitcase for the chili dog sauce: a gift to me more rare than a '59 Buick. Today in Atlanta, it's Michigan weather, cold and dull, darkening at dinnertime—like when Daddy would arrive from work, brushing snow off his wool coat. Once he brought us leftovers from the jukebox—in the stack of 45s, shiny as our patent leather shoes, we found *Love Potion Number 9!* His mustard-stained white shirt always reeked of onions spiked with cigarette smoke, grease, French fries. When he took off his sweaty shoes, Pico, our Chihuahua, rubbed her body crazily against them, then against his socks with their old potato odor. We loved the food smells at Angelo's but not the mishmash Daddy wore home—even in his moustache and the sticky sheen of his forehead as he kneeled to our level. When Mom handed him his cold Coke, he passed it around to each kid for a sip, though five sips nearly drained the six-ounce bottle.

—Karen Paul Holmes

Craft Tip #24: The *cynghanedd:* Welsh Poetics

—Marjory Wentworth

I have struggled against writing blank verse for as long as I can remember. When I was in graduate school, I felt like the only poet not writing in blank verse. I tried it with almost every poem I wrote, but it just never felt right. It felt as if I were writing against the grain, but I couldn't figure out why. I wanted fewer stresses and shorter lines, but I couldn't find a form that sounded quite right.

I was a semi-professional dancer for decades, which means that for most of my waking hours I was counting in eights. Since most of my experience was as a jazz dancer, there was a lot of syncopation and slight variation, but my inner metronome was and still is a variation of counting, singing, and literally breathing in counts of eight. Despite this dance background and studying music theory when I was considering choreography as a profession, my poetry lacked music. This really bothered me. It never dawned on me to directly link the way I already heard music with the poems I was writing.

Fortunately, I am friends with poet/novelist Ron Rash, who is the master of his interpretation of the *cynghanedd*. There are many variations of this often overlooked Welsh poetic form, but in much of Rash's work it is comprised of a 7-syllable line which yields an astonishing lyric intensity. The word literally means *harmony*, and the focus is on sound arrangement within a line; this play within the line requires a rich alliteration and attention to sound that creates a kind of echoing across the lines, what Hopkins referred to as *chiming*.

Rash, who has a Welsh background, discovered the ancient form of Welsh poetry when he was studying Welsh poetics. In order to increase the lyric intensity of his narrative poems, he began using the *cynghanedd*. I may or may not be a little Welsh, but I can tell you that this form is one I return to over and over again. I strongly suggest you try this form when you are writing a narrative poem, or if you are simply trying to get more music into your poetry. It frees you up to play with sound within and across the lines in ways that will astonish you. Take Ron Rash's "The Corpse Bird." Notice the internal rhyme: *call, fall, pall*; then *tightened* and *light* and *night*; and later *kin* and *coffin*.

> Bed-sick she heard the bird's call
> fall soft as a pall that night
> quilts tightened around her throat,
> her gray eyes narrowed, their light
> gone as she saw what she'd heard
> waiting for her in the tree
> cut down at daybreak by kin
> to make the coffin, bury
> that perch around her so death
> might find one less place of rest.

My strength is imagery and this heightened attention to repeated sound has really helped my poetry. One of my first attempts at a *cynghanedd* was a short poem called "Newlyweds." I knew the form was working for me in terms of the music when a young composer named Nathan Jones contacted me because he was interested in composing a choral piece based on the poem. I gave him permission, and about a half a year later the piece was performed by the Westminster Choir during Spoleto Festival USA. I met Nathan during a rehearsal, and it was like meeting an old friend. I am so fortunate, because Nathan continues to use my poetry as a source of inspiration. Listening to the choral piece was one of the most moving experiences of my life. It was like listening to angels singing my poem, and I was moved to tears.

> A bride beneath a backpack
> bigger than her body, holds
> a vase of red and yellow
> roses in front of her heart.
> The groom, dragging a suitcase
> on wheels, hugs a shopping bag
> stuffed with still-wrapped gifts,
> wedding cake balanced on top.
> They run through the airport,
> ribbons spilling thin white streams
> through the air behind them.

Poem and Prompt

Rimas Dissolutas at Chacala Beach

Not waving but drowning
—Stevie Smith

Not even your hand reaching from the past as you go down
into the Atlantic keeps me from the sea. Pacific waves like trucks
crash down on me, my legs tugged away in an avalanche of sand.
Sometimes I fall, suck in a snatch of salty air
and skid into the cave of the next wave, only to be hauled
back to the tideline with bottle caps, shells and small green beads.

With an arm raised, that visual cliché, is not how you went down
I'm sure—it's how *we* went down in the pool at Black Rock:
leggy ten-year-olds each holding her nose with one hand
and reaching up with the other in that mocking gesture of despair.
Down we went, face to face, our hair loosing small
bubbles as it streamed upwards and we stared like mermaids

into that liquid underworld, clear and paint blue, its only known
danger a dose of chlorine that left us headachy and pink-
eyed, our swimsuits smelling of hospital by the long day's end.
Did we sense then, as our lungs screamed for air
and our cheeks bulged with held breath, that this transparent wall
could surge into the hollows of our lungs and turn us to weed?

The fact is that after a while I couldn't stop. Rhythmically, alone,
I surged up, grabbed a mouthful of air and sank,
my arm marking the spot in a drama that would never end.
As it turned out, it was a kind of defiance of the future
as it is now of the past when I breast the Pacific, ignoring the call
of your hand in the air as Atlantic swells cover your head.

—Judith Barrington

This poem is written in a form known as *rimas dissolutas*. This form's single strict rule pertains to the rhyme pattern. Each line in the first stanza must end with a new sound. The pattern of sounds in that first stanza becomes the pattern for subsequent stanzas. The first line in each stanza must rhyme with the first line of all stanzas. The second line must rhyme with the second line of all stanzas, and so on.

Other than the rhyme pattern requirement, the form allows a lot of freedom. You can, for example, have as many stanzas as you like. You can determine how many lines in each stanza, though each stanza must have the same number of lines. Line lengths are up to the poet and may be uniform or variable.

Because Barrington has six lines in each stanza, she has six rhyming sounds. Your number of rhymes will depend on the number of lines in each of your stanzas.

The beauty of this form is the subtlety of the rhymes. Notice that Barrington has used some perfect rhymes, some near rhymes, and a few repeated words.

The poem must, of course, be about more than its rhymes. Read Barrington's poem aloud and listen for its other sound devices. Notice, too, the serious content of the poem, a death by drowning. Notice the circular structure. Notice the imagery, similes, and metaphors.

Your assignment is to write your own *rimas dissolutas*. Begin with a line you love and go from there. Follow the rhyme pattern from stanza to stanza.

Sample Poems

Of Clocks and Love

The radio reports conceptions of time—
that two clocks traveling at different speeds
can vary by seconds, minutes and hours.
Physicists surf waves on cosmic oceans.

A poet poor in math, I feel stymied
when scientists operate by creeds
near to religion, aiming telescopic power
to digitize mysteries of creation—

as the universe expands, space/time
swirls in a blender, milky ways bleed
ancient fires, one black hole devours
another. What simple harmonic motion

set off this wild yo-yo we call sublime?
4.3 babies are born every minute. I meet
with joy a great-grandson—and with fears
of drought-shriveled fruits, earthquake implosion.

Still, I cross off calendar days, set a time
the radio sings me awake. Little one, reach
out your arms to those who will adore
the beauty of your body/soul's creation.

—Charlotte Mandel

The Woods Are Open to Me Now

After hearing from my doctor

The woods are open to me now.
Nothing to fear in the leaf bed,
there are no *monstrous reveries*
to curdle my muscle or bone.

The woods now inspire a new vow,
of accepting the path ahead.
Nothing hiding behind a tree.
Nothing seeping beneath a stone.

With no fear in the woods, I plow
on through the terrors I once fled.
The dark can no longer take me
to the tightness I felt alone.

I push aside a low pine bough
with new thoughts forming in my head.
No more plunge into misery.
I know now, I'm on my way home.

—Ellie O'Leary

The Poet on the Poem: Alessandra Lynch

Magnolia

A wedding broke out in the magnolia—
        fever of white gloves, distressed wind.

The bells hung upside down. They'd choked
on their own tongues.
                                Hung too, on unspeaking terms
with the air, I acknowledged the impasse—
                I wore a dress of paralysis.

Then all her little white dresses lifted as one—
        as though on signal—a four year old
                girl tilting up her own dress in the living room, opening up
                like an umbrella to her mother's lover, her face, god, I can't
                even imagine it, sweet and cold, methodical, desperate,
trying to woo him—.

                        Maybe I don't want

a voice at all. All this mouthing in the magnolia—
thin cries
                —too delicate
                        to tend.

I think of a sea and its glistening foams and cascades hundreds of miles off
and its whales' limbic thudding through water, their intelligent eyes
bright with salt.
                Rushed wind...
                        White rushing petals...
                                                the ransacked
air.

DS: What ignited this poem? How did you get from the tree to the opening metaphor?

AL: When I write poetry, I work associatively (and swiftly) through image and sound. I never know what will arise from my tapping into language and tinkering with images. I read every draft obsessively to heed the music. I never analyze what I'm doing until several drafts later. In this way, I feel I can trust that what appears on the page is coming from a deeper, more surprising place—the realm of poetry—than what my conscious mind alone might conjure.

Living just outside my bedroom window, there is a magnolia tree that blooms yearly—roughly five days' worth of luminous white blossoms (at times they appear to be floating on air, detached from the branches). It grows so close to my window that it seems to be pressing into the room.

This magnolia is a tree I turn to when I am despondent, a tree I marvel over for its leaves' depth of glossy green, its supple blossoms' ghostly glow. One day, I began marveling over how the blossoms looked like thin white gloves, the whole tree like a wedding party or a bride of sorts—hence, the wedding metaphor in the poem. I felt distress in the tree, too, for a number of possible reasons: the wind was harrying the tree, magnolia blossoms last briefly, and my associations with *wedding* are based mainly on my experience as a child of my parents' harrowing divorce.

DL: I'm intrigued by your metaphor, *I wore a dress of paralysis.* Tell us about this metaphor and the surprising shift from the dress to the four-year-old girl and then to the whales.

AL: Perhaps *dress of paralysis* arose from the initial wedding metaphor—with its white gloves, but it also embodies the speaker's inability to express, to break out of the impasse and to move words and/or life forth.

All her little white dresses lifted as one opens a space or door into memory, expressing some kind of vulnerability—I feel the line as mysterious and ghostly. That scene of the little girl flirting with her mother's lover, *tilting up her own dress*, is a voiceless communication, a plea borne of a complex situation having to do with need and confusion.

The shift in the poem to the sea and its *glistening foams and cascades* is the speaker's way of contending with the enormous responsibility and ensuing futility expressed in *too delicate to tend*. The speaker adjusts her focus to the sea, the realm of whales. She might find respite and comfort at this point in the beauty and power and distance of the sea and the whales, but the wind lives everywhere—land and sea; here it disrupts this lulling sea-rhapsody, returning the speaker and the poem to the tree.

DL: The sounds in your poem are lovely and subtle. For example, in stanza 2, you have *hung* and its repetition in *tongues* and *unspeaking*. In stanza 3, you have *impasse*, *dress*, and *paralysis*. How deliberate was your use of assonance and consonance?

AL: My first drafts tend to be rife with imagery and music—it's how my mind works. It's how I've always invoked my poems. There's nothing particularly deliberate about it—all of it's unbidden. The music in language is visceral and mysterious and the truest mode of expression I know. All those sound sequences arose as I wrote the initial draft and they remained throughout the drafting process. I had many other moments of music that weren't as charged or intrinsic to the piece that I left behind on the cutting room floor (after doffing my hat to the work those lyrical passages helped me do). The music in language leads my mind, and I try my best to follow it and to recognize when the music is intrinsic to the image and to the emotional root of the poem versus when the music is decorative or just music for music's sake (though, at times, poems need moments of the latter, too).

DL: What is the function of your poem's form? At what point in the drafting did you incorporate the indentations?

AL: Fairly early in the drafting, I began indenting without consciously thinking about why or how—it just helped me feel a certain energy or life on the page. Now I see that I was probably following the feeling of agitation and augmenting the motif of air through the spaces. The indentations could also embody the expansion and contraction of breath in a distressed state or the structure or design of how magnolia blossoms appear on each branch. In earlier drafts, the indentation was more erratic and perhaps a bit melodramatic.

DL: In the closing stanza, with its three quick images, you return to the wind of the first stanza. Why that circling back? What made you decide to put the word *air* on its own line flush to the left margin?

AL: On some level, I might have wanted to keep the magnolia and all that it represents alive to the reader. Maybe the speaker was compelled (however unwittingly) to continue facing the manifestations of her current distress. She swerved off to marvel over the whales, but in swerving, she dropped into the sea, realm of the unconscious, realm of deep inner truths. Maybe those eyes were the catalyst for her to return and confront her own pain and bewilderment again for a truer catharsis.

In terms of the last few breaths of the poem, I kept fiddling with the placement of *air* before deciding to keep it flush to the left margin. I wanted the feeling of *ransacking* to reverberate with all the other elements of the poem before settling on *air*. Also, rhythmically, it felt too abrupt to have *air* on the same line as *ransacking*. And there was a sort of abandoned or neglected or stifled feeling I think I conveyed by isolating *air* in its own corner.

Ultimately, my writing process—including decisions about spacing and line breaks—is guided by intuition, not a whole lot of consciousness or deliberation. As Theodore Roethke said, *We think by feeling. What is there to know?*

Bonus Prompt: Syllabic Verse Poem

Syllabic verse has a fixed number of syllables per line, regardless of the number of stresses.

Sylvia Plath was fond of this form. Here is an excerpt from her poem "Mushrooms." Notice that each line consists of five syllables:

> We are shelves, we are
> Tables, we are meek,
> We are edible,
>
> Nudgers and shovers
> In spite of ourselves.
> Our kind multiplies:

For your own syllabic poem, choose a vegetable as your subject.

Determine how many syllables per line. You might write your first line and let that line's number of syllables set the pattern for the rest of the poem.

Use the first person point of view, singular or plural, so that your poem is a kind of dramatic monologue or persona poem.

As you become proficient with syllabic verse, you might want to challenge yourself to try a pattern of alternating the number of syllables per line, for example: 8-6-8-6, and so on.

IX. Expanding the Material

I keep writing about the ordinary because for me it's the home of the extraordinary, the only home.

—Philip Levine

Craft Tip #25: Poetic Sequences: Practice Makes Potential

—Oliver de la Paz

A significant inspirational experience happened to me during the summer of 2003 when I visited Barcelona, Spain. The Picasso Museum in Barcelona is a marvelous place because a visitor can get a sense of the ever-evolving perspective of the artist. Not only do you see Picasso's famous cubist paintings and the paintings from his Blue Period, you see his obsessive impulses, his attempts at other media, his drafts.

One gallery showroom in the Picasso Museum struck my fancy. Housed within a vast room, with twenty-foot high ceilings, paintings similar in color, texture, and subject matter occupied every wall of the room. There were even tables at the center of the room dedicated to the artist's sketchbooks. In a series of fifty-eight oil paintings inspired by *Las Meninas* by Velázquez, Picasso performed an elaborate study of technique, color, and form.

In that extensive series, Picasso played with perspective, shifting the dimensions of some of the subjects contained within the larger canvas, yet keeping the integrity of the subject intact. What fascinated me most about *Las Meninas* was how Picasso took a subject matter like Valázquez's painting, studied it obsessively by re-painting the component parts of the larger piece, and thus created an immense volume of distinct pieces that combine into a larger concept.

The idea of a poetic sequence for me, then, is analogous to what Picasso attempted in his study of *Las Meninas*. By writing a series or sequence of poems on a singular subject, we can create a volume of individual poems that are at once independent and in dialogue with adjacent poems in the series or sequence. These are generative exercises—painting studies and sequential writing. They create volumes of work with a premium on volume. I know that I may not be creating my finest poem, but I also know that there's a bigger picture. As you're writing sequences, it's always important to keep the bigger picture in mind.

I've got two takes on what working in a poetic sequence grants me as an artist. My intellectual side values that the poetic sequence allows for a close and obsessive study of a single subject. By visiting and revisiting a subject, I'm able to study each angle, flaw, embellishment, and groove. I'm able to catch the ways shadows are cast differently at different times of day. Or the way my personal tonal, dictated by my day's events, shifts or alters the way I see myself in the poems I make.

My practical side values the relief I feel when I don't have to mine for a new subject. I'm a father of three children, a husband, and a fidget with administrative and academic duties. It is quite difficult to navigate new terrain when it comes to seeking materials for subject matter and I've found that working in sequences frees me from obsessing over a blank page. Psychologically, I'm prepared to work with content that has already been worked over.

To be even more practical, I use a few tricks or techniques over and over again to guide me as I write my sequences:

1. I unify my sequences through titles. For example, I have a sequence or a series of "Self-Portrait with..." poems in my most recent book, *Requiem for the Orchard*. In my second book, I have a number of "Aubade with..." poems.

2. I generate discrepancies in the sequences through titles as well. Again, I refer to *Requiem for the Orchard* where I have a poem entitled "Self-Portrait with Taxidermy" and another entitled "Self-Portrait with a Spillway." While the "Self-Portrait" part of the title identifies the poems as being part of a sequence, the second part of the title creates the change or shift.

3. I use a recurring word, color, animal, or image throughout the sequences. Birds are prevalent in a number of my book projects. So is the word *dark*.

4. I steal lines and cadences from myself and rework them.

5. I give myself a finite amount of time to work on each poem in a sequence. Mind you, I'm only talking about compositionally, not in terms of revision. I find that if I give myself too much time to write a new poem in any given sequence, the poem begins to assert its own identity outside of that sequence. This is neither bad nor good. If you look at Picasso's *Las Meninas* studies, his paintings are never complete.

6. I remind myself that I will come back to the poem and that the poem is working in conversation with other poems from the series. This is key.

I reiterate, there is a bigger picture when it comes to writing in a sequence. It's a way to handle obsessive material as well as a time-crunch.

Poem and Prompt

Hummingbird

You vent a riff of high clicks
like a dollhouse door creaking as it
swings unlatched in a model
of wind. Unlike me, you can sing
and fly at the same time.
Sucker for a touch of honey
in the water, you small marvel,
great unbumbling bee, you are more

brazen than the winged
idols of gold that brought endless
song to Byzantium and the mind
of Yeats. Hmm: more miracle
than bird, yet not once out of nature.
The faster you can fly from
the unnatural, the more fearless
you are, anything but delicate.

Today in a wood I'm stilled
by majesty unimagined. You light
within reach, cooling wings
at a trickle of water over crystal
charms that someone has set
on a mossy stone. Here you are
drinking, thinking me, in my dull
green shirt, just another small tree.

—A. E. Stringer

The title of Stringer's praise poem names his subject. The first line begins with apostrophe. This direct address to the hummingbird is maintained throughout the poem. As is typical in a praise poem, Stringer uses hyperbole: the hummingbird is a *small miracle* and a *great unbumbling bee* and is *more // brazen than the winged / idols of gold that brought endless / song to Byzantium and the mind / of Yeats*. The allusion to Yeats and his "Sailing to Byzantium" works to elevate the significance of the hummingbird.

I admire the poem's tone which Stringer achieves through a variety of techniques. The direct address creates a feeling of intimacy. The hyperbole creates a feeling of reverence as well as playfulness. The reverence is enhanced with elegant diction such as *delicate* and *majesty*. The playfulness is enhanced by colloquial language, e.g., *Sucker for a touch of honey* and *Hmm*. There's also a touch of humor in the poem as the speaker compares himself to the hummingbird and declares that *Unlike me, you can sing / and fly at the same time*, a spin on the walk-and-chew-gum-at-the-same-time cliché.

Stringer makes rich use of imagery. Notice how many senses are appealed to in just the first stanza: sound (*clicks, creaking*), taste (*touch of honey*), and motion (*swings, fly*). In the final stanza we have the stillness of the speaker as he observes the motions of the hummingbird, the *cooling wings / at a trickle of water*, and the *mossy stone*. Note especially the image that closes the poem as the speaker imagines the bird mistaking him in his *dull / green shirt* for *just another small tree*.

Stringer gives his poem a somewhat formal structure of three stanzas, each consisting of eight lines. This seems appropriate for a praise poem.

For your own praise poem, first choose a subject from nature. This might be a different kind of bird, a rodent, insect, flower, vegetable, or tree. Do not choose a person.

Before you begin drafting, brainstorm a list of your subject's virtues. Others may come to you later.

As you begin your draft, use apostrophe, speaking directly to your subject. But also keep the speaker present in the poem. Make us aware of him or her as observer.

Work in the virtues. Use some hyperbole in describing them. Mix elegant diction with colloquial diction.

Include some imagery. Try to appeal to several different senses. See if you can end with an image that reveals what the subject thinks of the speaker—a difficult challenge, but try it.

As you revise, work on achieving a strong tone. Do we hear the speaker's voice? Does your poem elicit powerful feelings in the reader? Is there some variety in the feelings?

Include some formal elements in your poem's structure.

Sample Poems

October Sunrise

Here you are again, the same rosy-fingered dawn
who opened ten years' worth of days during the Trojan War,
and then ten more on Odysseus' return to Ithaka
as he sailed around and across the wine-dark sea.
Now, eons later you still appear each morning,
to wake ordinary neighborhoods not known for epic greatness,
stealing in so quietly, quieter even than the muffled thud
of a newspaper landing on someone's sidewalk or steps.
As if on signal, out goes the yellow rectangle of window across the street,
on comes the glow of October treetops: towering amber maples,
and closer to the ground, smaller pink vibernums and juneberries,
reflecting the soft colors that spread slowly across the horizon.
Roofs and windshields of cars parked along the curb,
skinny bicycles chained to lamp posts bordering the parkway,
a red stop sign, yellow caution signs, neon joggers all capture
that first light, hold it, and send it back out into the early air.
And for those few minutes at daybreak,
until harsher light arrives to bear witness,
you, rosy dawn, belie our own Homeric struggles, small and big,
with your sunrise gift: one sweet momentary illusion of peace.

—Susan Gundlach

Ode to Tulsi

*Tulsi is Holy Basil, which is worshipped by
Hindus and has several medicinal uses.*

Your astringent nip shocks all,
yet you seem unaware of it
as you stand serenely,
your green radiating
sky and bricks around you.

As women circumambulate you,
they begin to call you their dearest friend.
Glamorous on your pedestal,
you are like the spirit in stones
and trees that knows human touch.

You are confetti flung by handfuls
on gods during worship.
Perfuming desserts, gifts, waters
sipped by gods and humans, you rival
the snaking smoke of incense,
you usurp shrines.

You perfume nuptial beds, dot milk
and honey fed to every married pair.
Chefs who yearn for novelty easily
turn to you, as do teetotalers, artists,
cultists, landscapers, and the very gods
whose throne you have claimed.
No one can wage war against you
since you are mute; you only invite
song and breath.

—Pramila Venkateswaran

Craft Tip #26: Expanding the Territory

—Martha Collins

For the last ten or fifteen years, I've been incorporating research into my poetry. Not that I haven't always looked up things when I needed to; the poignant or strange fact has always seemed to me as meaningful an element in poetry as the revered image, and I've always checked my facts.

But when I saw an exhibit of lynching postcards and discovered that the *hanging* my father had mentioned seeing as a child was actually a *lynching*, I found myself unable to put that particular fact out of my mind. Finally, I realized, I had to do some major research. First I googled *lynching* and the victim's name; then I googled *Cairo, Illinois*, where the lynching took place; then I googled names and topics suggested by what I had googled. I read numerous articles and books; I wrote to people whose names I found online; I visited Cairo four times and explored the library, the museum, and the town itself. The result of my research was *Blue Front*, a book-length poem based on a lynching my father witnessed when he was five years old.

While writing that long poem, I so forgot about myself that I once thought I was in Cairo when I wasn't. Even now, writing about a somewhat later time for another book, I find myself saying 1915 instead of 2015.

Which is all to the (poetic) good. *Anybody who has survived his childhood has enough information about life to last him the rest of his days*, said Flannery O'Connor—a statement I often cite and thoroughly agree with. But there comes a time, for some of us, when our sense of ourselves and our hurting world may call out for a move beyond that information.

For me, moving beyond has not meant leaving behind. A poet I know saw the lynching postcard exhibit and said he'd tried to write about it but hadn't been able to. Well, I said, I couldn't have written about it either if I hadn't had some personal connection to it.

It was thinking about that connection that led me to encourage poets to expand their own poetic territory by doing research. Not just any research: I want to emphasize the importance of having some personal relation to the material.

Here's a series of questions you can use to move towards writing your own poems that combine the personal and the historical. Use it quickly the first time around; you can always go back and fill in. And then move on.

1. Write down the name of the place where you were born and, if different, significant places where you lived as a child. Name something of historical significance that happened in each of these places. And, if you can, name at least one person who lived in each place who became known outside the local community.

2. Where was your mother born? Where did she grow up? When did she or her ancestors come to North America? Are there any family stories that might relate in a more general way to historical events that she or other family members have spoken of?

3. Same questions as in #2 for your father.

4. Name one historical figure you admire. Name one you don't admire, but who nonetheless intrigues you.

5. Name, if you can, one somewhat obscure historical figure who interests you.

6. Name a scientific area, discovery, or pursuit that interests you.

7. Name two deceased artists (writers, musicians, painters, etc.) who interest you.

8. If you could go back to a period in history prior to your birth, what would it be?

9. What is the most obscure subject you know something about?

10. Name a subject that you have always wanted to know more about.

11. Name an animal, tree, flower, river, mountain or other natural being, object, or place that interests you.

12. Shut your eyes. Let your mind wander through the events of recent weeks as recorded in the media until you find an image or group of words. Do not aim for importance; look for something specific that has stuck with you.

The wealth of information you uncover in responding to these questions may very well be the impetus to a series of short poems or a long narrative poem in which you find a personal connection to something historical.

Poem and Prompt

Theory of Lipstick

Coral is far more red than her lips' red...
—William Shakespeare

Pot rouge, rouge pot, glosser, lip plumper, bee
stung devil's candy and painted porcelain
Fire and Ice, a vermillion bullet,
dangerous beauty lipstick, carmine death rub, history
of henna. Fact: more men get lip cancer

because they don't wear lipstick or butter
jumble of a luminous palette with brush made
to outlast, last long, kiss off, you ruby busser,
your gilded rose bud bluster is weapon and wine.
QE's blend: cochineal mixed with egg, gum Arabic

and fig milk—alizarin crimson and lead—poison
to men who kiss women wearing lipstick, once illegal
and loathsome—then cherry jelly bean licked and smeared,
then balm gloss crayon, a cocktail of the mouth,
happy hour lip-o-hito, lip-arita, with pout-fashioned chaser

made from fruit pigment and raspberry cream,
a lux of shimmer-shine, lipstick glimmer, duo
in satin-lined pouch, Clara Bow glow: city brilliant
and country chick—sparkling, sensual, silks
and sangria stains, those radiant tints and beeswax liberty—

oh, kiss me now, oh, double agents of beauty
slip me essential pencils in various shades
of nude and pearl and suede, oh, bombshell lipstick,
sinner and saint, venom and lotsa sugar, lip sweet,
pucker up gelato: every pink signal is a warning.

—Karla Huston

Huston gathered the information for this poem from a book on the history of lipstick. One of the poem's many pleasures is the opulence of its details—the numerous synonyms for lipstick, the different kinds of lipstick, and the variety of lipstick colors. The poem consists of a series of lists or catalogs. In the midst of the lists is a fact (line 5), which is identified as such, and two recipes (lines 10-11, line 16). Note, too, the heavy use of sentence fragments and their contribution to the poem's feeling of speed.

Be sure to read this poem aloud. Its diction is a pleasure to speak. Bountiful alliteration gives the poem a wonderful music and pace, e.g., *painted porcelain, history of henna, bud bluster, weapon and wine,* and *sparkling, sensual, silks / and sangria stains.*

Note the prevalence of words using plosive letters (p, t, k, b, d, g). These letters make their words pop out of the mouth. Many of Huston's words employ the letter *p*: *pot, lip, plumper, painted, lipstick.* Many employ the letter *b*: *bee, bullet, beauty, because, butter, jumble, ruby busser.* You could make a similar list of words with any of the six plosives.

Huston also employs a number of words with fricatives (f, s, v, z). Note the plethora of *s* sounds: *stung, devil's, dangerous, history, luminous, bluster.* And the run of *f* sounds: *Fire, Fact, off, fry, fruit.* These also add to the poem's music and energy.

The poet corrals her material into five 5-line stanzas and makes it behave. She uses four colons which grab our attention and make us pause in the midst of the tumult. She closes the poem with an ecstatic direct address to lips and then a declarative statement.

For your own poem, begin with a title. Write down "Theory of _____."

Then fill in the blank. Perhaps Mushrooms, Roses, Tomatoes, Thimbles, Neckties, Knots, Wine, Galoshes. Do a Google search or go to Wikipedia and research your subject. Have paper and pen with you. Write down some history, some facts, descriptive details, wonderful words.

Now begin your draft. Pile on the information from your notes. Insert a fact and identify it as a fact. Be bold. You might want to vary the wording, e.g., *Esoteric information* instead of *Fact*, so as not to follow the model too closely. Be playful. Don't worry about achieving complete sentences or making exact sense.

As you revise your first draft, pay attention to diction. Consciously use plosives and fricatives. You don't need to use all of them, but sprinkle your poem with similar sounds. Go for an explosion of sounds.

Towards the end, zero in with a direct address, perhaps to your subject or to something closely related to it.

As you feel your poem getting close to done, plan a structure. Get some symmetry, e.g., four 4-line stanzas, six 6-line stanzas, twelve 2-line stanzas.

Sample Poems

Theory of Wine

Grape deflate, princess poison, ape maker of
flush face. Truth:
this drink's fruit is a rubber for the thumb.

When fermentation comes, it's over a barrel
in the vein's river styx,
a breathing mass of berried baubles,

the steward of God's blood undone,
unknowing the world's oldest shoe was found
in the world's oldest winery,

someone climbing the first *vinum*
to loft it and yard it, get really high off it.
The spirited stakes:

horse graze, bad egg, sweaty.
Hold of lush roses! Still of distillery!
More funk for the dump: cork taint,

forest-floor, vomit in reds.
Later, raisin paint, stomp mob, jug
of brain thuggery spun degree in drunk studies.

Dear crush, dear club, dear
happiest hour, let me count casks,
large bowls with small stems

to toast ruined perfume, my overloud voice
on the concord cruise, my lips'
disdain with your bruise and bloom.

—Angela Vogel

Theory of Male Crickets

With grasshoppers and katydids for cousins,
your Gryllidae family thrives worldwide.

Though kept in cages for good luck by some,
deep-fried for dinner by others,

and noted in poems by Wordsworth and Keats,
you march on to your own drum.

Born in the spring, you molt ten times
before you turn on and seek mates.

You hide during dangerous days,
and scrape serrated forewings in the dark.

On fall nights, with you under leaves
and shrubs, my world turns jungle.

One of your calls challenges nearby males,
and I envision your lashing antennae,

flaring mandibles, and fierce grappling—
armored knights jousting over love.

Another call courts females, and, after
each coupling, your song shifts to triumph.

No longer stuck on one steady staccato,
I listen for the melody riff, your ode to joy.

You can sing me to sleep or keep me awake,
your chirps laying bare what you're up to.

—Jeanie Greensfelder

Craft Tip #27: Writing from Photographs: A Poetic Sequence

—Susan Rich

For two years, I attempted to write poems inspired by the book, *The Magic Box: The Eccentric Genius of Hannah Maynard,* by Claire Weissman Wilks, a book I discovered one Thanksgiving weekend in a secondhand bookstore. For two years, I failed. The drafts remained half-written on the page. I abandoned them because I couldn't find a way to write the poems in a way that complemented such enigmatic photographs. And yet, I didn't want to give up. The images kept tugging at me.

The photographs stunned me: a woman's profile in a life-sized keyhole; a triad of women—each the same woman—pouring afternoon tea; an older woman posed with a wine decanter and cloud. I was looking at images that I had no vocabulary for, no experience deciphering. I turned the sepia-toned pages and looked at what might, in turn, have presaged the work of surrealist, avant-garde, and feminist photographers of the mid- and late-twentieth century. How could I take on such a project?

What I needed was a way to trick myself into being a better poet, a poet capable of working with these images. It's difficult to say what finally allowed me to write "The Dark Room" sequence other than building a larger capacity inside myself for letting go of expectation. Several of my drafts never made it beyond my notebook. I learned not to worry about the enormity of what I did not know about Hannah Maynard but instead enjoyed the unknowing.

Recently, at a Seattle Arts and Lectures interview, poet Mary Szybist confessed that bewilderment is her favorite emotion, a psychological space that she writes from. For me, I believe my best writing comes from an obsessive curiosity mixed with abject fear. This heightened energy keeps me going beyond the single poem. Working on a poetic sequence allows me to stretch out and investigate more than I can do in one piece. For example, Hannah Maynard created self-portraits, trick photographs featuring her nephew sawed in half, and strange still lifes. I needed more space than one poem could hold for my responses. I wanted to write from many different perspectives.

It turns out that I like to write not only about what I can see but also about what I cannot see. In ekphrastic poetry (work that takes its inspiration from another work of art) the image works as an emotional anchor. The photograph I begin with functions as a readymade rough draft. If the photographer's work sparks my curiosity (and fear!), I begin to research her portfolio of work. Looking at nineteenth-century photographs takes me away from the dailiness of my own life and into something larger. Over time it seems I can inhabit the art and life of a woman photographer, even one born one hundred years before me. We both know what it feels like to stand alone in a dark room to create art.

Tips for Writing Sequences from Photographs:

1. Let each photograph be a launch pad, not a prison for your ekphrastic poem.

2. What you don't know will lead you. Don't worry if you aren't a photo-historian.

3. Research the historical context of the time (technology, fashion, war).

4. Let yourself go beyond the images to discover the artist's life experiences.

5. Find out what cameras looked like at the time the picture was taken.

6. Think about what is happening just outside the frame.

7. Give yourself permission to take plenty of time; there's so much to explore.

8. Learn about the photographer's home, family, and education.

9. Examine the technical aspects of the work and then go beyond them.

10. Use the language of the photographer: *light, shadow, aperture, f-stop.*

To illustrate how these tips can be put to use, here's a poem from my "Dark Room" series:

Tricks a Girl Can Do

Hannah Maynard (1834-1918) was a Canadian photographer who created surreal images after the death of her daughter; she was a proto-surrealist.

I will hang myself in picture frames
in drawing rooms where grief
is not allowed a wicker chair

then grimace back at this facade
from umbrella eyes
under a cage of silvering hair.

Look! I've learned to slice myself in three
to sit politely at the table
with ginger punch and teacake;

offer thin-lipped graves
of pleasantries. I develop myself
in the pharmacist's chemicals

three women I'm loathe to understand—
presences I sometimes cajole
into modern light and shadow.

We culminate in a gelatin scene—
a daughter birthed from a spiral shell,
a keyhole tall enough to strut through.

Poem and Prompt

A Full Sentence of Paint

after Pelvis IV *by Georgia O'Keeffe, 1944, oil on masonite*

On her way to the sun, she meets a scavenger hawk
circling the leftover shadow of a lone hip.

A clock chimes inside the woman's blue season.

The canvas of sky stretches taut. One hand folds
onto the left side of her bent body, wrinkling into bone.

She paints the syntax of paint:
a boundless vowel of blue and the mute reason of white.

She is soaked in a flat mountain of sage.
Centuries are skylines of suggestion.

After three attempts,
she paints the edges first, bone hole last.

On a boat of blue churning through juniper, she floats
out of the picture and into the razored sound of the sun.

Tubes of indigo draw out half-night.

She hikes back through miles of cow hips and elm roots,
wearing the dirty blouse of the sun.

The moon is shaded, but whole in the basin of bone.

—Lauren Camp

Lauren Camp gives us an ekphrastic poem, in this instance, one stimulated by a painting. She lets us know in an informational note that the scene she describes was influenced by a Georgia O'Keeffe painting. Her method is to allow her speaker to observe the painter at work. The speaker follows O'Keeffe as the painter finds a bone in the desert and pulls additional materials from the setting—the plants, the sun, the sky, the color blue.

There are several intriguing elements to the poem, beginning with the title. A *sentence* of paint? Perhaps Camp is suggesting that painting has its own language, its own syntax. Then what is that clock that chimes in line 3 *inside the woman's blue season*? And the *razored sound of the sun*? And the *dirty blouse of the sun*? Rather than feeling put off by these enigmatic metaphors, I am intrigued by them. They keep pulling me back to the poem.

Let's do an ekphrastic poem. First find a painting or photograph that captures your imagination.

Once you've chosen your piece, study it carefully. Observe its center, its edges, textures, colors. Are people in it? Any trees, flowers, furniture?

Write a quick prose description and/or list of details.

Consider using one of these approaches to your poem:

1. Imagine yourself observing the artist at work.

2. Consider the effect of the artwork on your speaker.

3. Observe someone else observing and responding to the artwork.

4. Focus on a limited aspect of the work, e.g., the bottle of wine on a fully laden table.

5. Enter the artwork and become part of the scene.

6. Consider what is left out of the artwork.

Now begin a draft. Bring in your description and list of details. If your artwork is dominated by a particular color, weave that color in and out of your poem. If there are multiple colors, bring them in. Of course, your poem should be rich in imagery. You are painting a picture with words. Let your imagination be stimulated by the artwork.

Allow a few enigmatic metaphors to enter the poem. Don't be excessively literal.

After several drafts, zero in on a form for your poem. Do you want a single stanza? Alternating stanza lengths as Camp has? Couplets? Quatrains? Experiment until the form seems just right.

Beneath your title, add a note to identify the artist and the artwork.

Sample Poems

Cartwheel, far flight, pirouette

Wheat Fields at Auvers Under Clouded Sky
—Van Gogh

A sort of high church glossolalia
in the many steepled wheat—to me

its rasping babble says, "mill stone, bones, bullets."

Each day the sun ground to grit becomes
a Braille for those blind to light. I paint it

again and again and still they don't see
what I see. With all I've got, I am

hallooing tools. I am bruised-blooming school.

With this wheat, I am never alone. I
brush blue seeking. I am the Dutch Degas

dance-chancing, scaffold-less ultramarine sigh.

Clouds mark the quiet slide of time. I must
have the engraver's patience, do one bright thing.

If only this chanting wheat might be for me
small votives praying a path into the dark

where I might thrash free of my odd chaff
and shine cartwheel, far flight, pirouette,

starlight.

—Paula Schulz

The Funeral of Shelley

Edouard Fournier. Oil on canvas, 1889

I prefer the painting's fictive depiction
to the gruesome reality.
Something about the poet's early tragic
death being what was really important.
Shelley, life-like, as though asleep
on the crematory pyre at shoreline,
Mary kneeling in the background.
But it wasn't so.
                              When washed up
that summer day, his bloated body
was unrecognizable—no face, no hands.
Italian law mandated a blanketing of lime,
immediate burial in the sand. Weeks later,
it took an hour and a long trench to locate,
excavate him on the day of his cremation—
a metal furnace lugged out to the beach.
                              Leigh Hunt, grief-stricken,
remained in the coach; poor Byron
soon wandered off and swam to his boat,
the *Bolivar,* getting badly sunburned—
his Shelley gone, "the *best* and least selfish
man I ever knew," he said. Mary Shelley
wasn't there. Trelawney plucked his friend's
carbonized heart from the ashes,
later gave it to her.

I like how the artist made the story his:
the bleak winter scene, muted colors,
gray somber tones of sky, water,
windswept beach; the black waiting carriage;
the mourners—among them Trelawny, Hunt,

and Byron in dramatic grieving poses;
the wretched bundled branches.
Smoke blows toward and beyond
a distant wide and high horizon line.

—Wanda Praisner
published in *The Kelsey Review*

The Poet on the Poem: Chana Bloch

Happiness Research

Rain over Berkeley! The birds are all out
delivering the news.
The evening is wet and happy tonight.
"Is there more to happiness than feeling happy?"
the moral philosophers inquire.

Research has shown
if you spot a dime on the sidewalk
you're more likely to tell the professor your life
is fine, thank you. The effect
generally lasts about twenty minutes.

Scientists are closing in on
the crowded quarter of the brain
where happiness lives. They like to think
it's hunkered down
in the left prefrontal cortex.

"Even in the slums of Calcutta
people on the street describe themselves
as reasonably happy." Why not be
reasonable? why not in Berkeley? why not
right now, sweetheart, while the rain
is stroking the roof?

The split-leaf philodendron is happy
to be watered and fed.
The dress I unbuttoned is more than glad
to be draped on the chair.

DL: Research is clearly an important motif in your poem. How much actual research went into the writing of the poem? Which came first, the science or the love poem?

CB: Over the past two decades research on happiness by social scientists, neuroscientists, and psycho-pharmacologists has grown at a phenomenal rate. I must admit that I can't help reading the stuff. So it was not by chance that I clipped and saved a review-article by Thomas Nagle in the *New York Review of Books*, "Who is Happy and When?" The moral philosopher Sissela Bok, who wrote the book under review, *Exploring Happiness: From Aristotle to Brain Science* (Yale UP), wants to know: What is happiness? How much should we value it? Questions I've often thought about.

I almost said that science came before love in writing this poem, but when I looked at the article again, I saw the illustration that first caught my attention—Rubens' captivating portrait of himself and his young wife, *In the Honeysuckle Bower*, painted the year of their marriage. In both faces, the lineaments of gratified desire.

DL: What do you see as the function of the two quotations you've woven into the poem?

CB: I hope the quotations will draw the reader into the poem, just as they drew me into the review. They made me ask myself: How am I doing on a scale of one to ten? Contented, elated, exhilarated? Which suggests that I was ready to appear in the poem long before I made my appearance.

In the version of "Happiness Research" I drafted a few years earlier, the scientists and the dime were already present, though not the inquiring professor. Sharing the page was *a Norwegian philosopher, 82, who recommends / daily swigs of cod liver oil / for despair*. That draft of the poem remained parked in a desk drawer until science and love revved up its engine.

DL: In stanza 4 you suddenly switch from third person point of view to a first person direct address to *sweetheart*. This and the rain *stroking the roof* move the poem from scientific to personal and intimate. At what point in your drafting did this risky shift enter the poem? How did you know it would work?

CB: Once I disposed of the cod liver oil and added the two quotes, the direction of the poem became clear. I knew I had the setting and the dramatis personae—our house (rain on the roof, a chair, and a split-leaf philodendron) and the two of us. I even had a come-hither line, which turns on the two senses of *reasonable*: the people in Calcutta are passably happy; let's you and I be sensible. *Why not be reasonable?* might conceivably sound irritated, even reproachful, but the context makes clear that it's playful, teasing, inviting. At that point I was more than glad to work on the poem. I was elated.

DL: You end the poem with a stunning sensual image. Tell us about your use of personification there, the dress that is *more than glad.*

CB: The dress, *c'est moi.* The truth is, I usually wore pants in those days, but a poem needn't be true to fact so long as it is true to experience.

When this poem was first published in *The Cortland Review*, it ended with the philodendron *doing its new green thing.* Once something is in print, I often can't help wanting to change it. While working on *Swimming in the Rain: New and Selected Poems, 1980-2015,* I decided that the happy plant was too nature-club-wholesome an ending for a seduction scene, so I revised and changed the order of the lines in order to end with the dress.

DL: Your first three stanzas each have five lines. Then you alter this pattern and give stanza 4 six lines and stanza 5 four lines. Why not stick to the established pattern?

CB: My poems often have an irregular number of lines in each stanza. Although I do write in couplets, triplets, or quatrains, I like to break the form depending on the demands of the poem. In stanza 4 I lay out my argument, so I need a little more room. And there's a reason, too, for the quick denouement in stanza 5: so the couple can get down to business.

Bonus Prompt: The Double Trouble Poem

Choose a topic that lends itself to a list, e.g., lost things, your fears, trees, favorite desserts, things you want, things you dislike, kinds of snakes.

Now write a quick ten-line poem. As you draft your poem, make each line a complete sentence. Leave an empty line after each written line.

Once the first draft is done, return to it and add a new line after every line in the draft.

Make each new line contain a rhyme or near-rhyme with a word in the preceding line. Your poem will thus be sound-driven. Rather than forcing end rhymes, scatter the rhymes throughout the lines.

Your draft will then be twenty lines.

X. Revision

Creativity is really the structuring of magic.

—Anne Kent Rush

Craft Tip #28: Sound Revision

—Tami Haaland

Listening to the sounds of vowels and consonants is one of my favorite revision methods. Of the two, consonants appear to be more dominant, the first to be recognized, but vowels in their variations and subtle differences can also affect the music of a poem and alter the mood for the reader.

One of my favorite poems to illustrate this point is Robert Hayden's "Those Winter Sundays." The initial lines highlight the *blueblack cold* of the unheated rooms in winter, *then with cracked hands that ached / from labor in the weekday weather* the speaker's father builds a fire and makes the *banked fires blaze.* The sounds are onomatopoetic, illustrating the snapping and stacking of wood, but further, they capture the discomfort of the situation, the coldness and severity of winter. After *the rooms were warm, he'd call, / and slowly I would rise and dress.* I love this shift from quick vowels and hard-stopped *c*'s and *b*'s, of *cracked hands...ached* and *banked fires blazed,* to the languid sounds after the fire is built and the teenaged son is stirring. Here, the vowels are longer and the *m* and *r* and *s* sounds linger in this pleasant warmth and slow movement of the son before the lines turn again to the *chronic angers of that house.*

In another example, the light and dark (though lightly dark) sounds in Christina Rossetti's "A Daughter of Eve" illustrate the effect word choice can have on tone. She uses primarily vowels made in the front of the mouth, short *i*'s and *a*'s, but even her long sounds, like *moon* and *fool,* seem to come forward because of the surrounding consonants. There is a lightness in these sounds and an elegance in the movement of the lines, made more effective by the form she uses. Despite the serious nature of her theme—that the speaker is *a daughter of Eve* because she has made a choice she regrets—the vowels demonstrate a brightness tempered by the slower, and perhaps cooler, contemplative nature of *moon* and *fool.*

Long, round sounds, which slow pronunciation, are equally delightful, but they are often more ponderous, like *hung down long yellow evil necks* in Roethke's "Florist's Root Cellar." If the reader takes the time to experience the vowels in this line, it is difficult to say them quickly, in part because the words also have those enduring beginning and ending sounds, like *h, n, ng,* and *l.* In a pleasant turn, the phrase snaps shut with *necks.*

It's not as if sound has inherent meaning. The sounds made in the front of the mouth, though they can move quickly and easily into the world, do not always pair with light and easy subjects, nor do the long and ponderous sounds at the back of the mouth always pair with heavy or dark subjects. The line from Roethke has a certain comedy about it, hyperbolic as it is, while Rossetti's poem, whose subject is more serious, presents itself with delicacy.

Sounds are one of the primary tools of poets, and in my own revision, I attend to sounds as a way of discovering where the poem might still go. I eliminate intervening and unnecessary words that sometimes block the avenue of sound. Listening to my own poem—reading it aloud and recording it—gets my ear involved and helps me revise for better sounds. My poems often begin with a certain amount of clutter, and while revision is many things, it is also a way of cleaning up the surface and testing the authenticity of each word to see and hear if it belongs.

Poem and Prompt

Birding at the Dairy

We're searching
for the single

yellow-headed
blackbird

we've heard
commingles

with thousands
of starlings

and brown-headed
cowbirds,

when the many-
headed body

arises
and undulates,

a sudden congress
of wings

in a maneuvering
wave that veers

and wheels, a fleet
and schooling swarm

in synchronous alarm,
a bloom radiating

in ribbons, in sheets,
in waterfall,

a murmuration
of birds

that turns
liquid in air,

that whooshes
like waves

on the shore,
or the breath

of a great
seething prayer.

—Sidney Wade

The speaker in the poem, a collective *We*, goes to a particular spot expecting to see a spectacular sight and gets one even more spectacular than anticipated. The long skinny form seems just right for a poem about how a multitude of birds lifts up off the ground and flies in single formation. Notice that the poem is one continuous sentence, punctuated correctly. The syntax keeps us moving forward; the short 2-line stanzas slow us down and allow a moment to breathe between stanzas.

I'm intrigued by the structural plan of this poem: *We were doing A when B occurred.* That's the frame of the poem. Wade then fills the frame with image after image and some metaphors which enable us to visualize the sight she is describing.

Notice the sound devices:

1. Double vowel words: *veers, wheels, fleet, schooling, bloom, sheets, whooshes, seething.* Notice the preponderance of *ee* and *oo* words and the long sounds that result when you read the poem aloud.

2. Scattered rhymes: *single, commingles, starlings, wings.* This kind of rhyme adds a lovely subtlety to the music of a poem.

3. Consonance: the *m* of *many-headed, maneuvering, swarm, alarm, bloom, murmuration*

4. Alliteration: the initial *w* of *we've, when, wave, wheels, waterfall, whooshes*

Your challenge is to first select some spectacular sight from Nature. We all have them. Then using the structural plan that Wade employs as well as the first person plural point of view, begin your draft. Describe, describe, describe. Keep asking yourself, What was that like? Keep mining your brain for strong details and images.

After you're a few drafts along, pore over the poem and enhance the sounds. Pay attention to the music of your verbs. Don't settle for the first ones that come to you; look for the best ones.

Have fun with the scattered rhyme device. Find a word you like, one that's in your draft and that sounds good to you. Brainstorm a list of rhyming words. Plug some of those words into your poem.

Capitalize on the natural music of our language by bringing in some consonance and alliteration.

When you revise for sound, you may very well surprise yourself into some new discoveries about your poem.

Sample Poems

Gull Watching at the Outer Banks

We are like posed statues in the park
They are like feathered kites

floating against the horizon
dipping and gliding
flapping and soaring

in near mid-
air collision

Like plumed, cloud-skimming
boomerangs

they veer
arc and circle

Seized by random currents
like air-borne fish

they dart, stream, and dive
lofted by updrafts—

they lilt and sway
beak to tail

Like fearless back-pedaling aerialists
criss-crossing in sky acrobatics—

they shift and swoop
beneath the clouds

then they land
on peaks and slants of weathered shingles

in pairs and singles
where they flout and strut about

and sneer at us below—
weighted down, anchored in sand.

—Kim Klugh

Kiva

this dark aperture
whole note in the dirt
moonless siren-song

this murmuring drum
this centripetal din
buried like thunder

this quickened pulse
rumble of earth
this drop of blood

this yawning maw
this mound-movement
of ants to a hole

this one-eyed world
humming like talismans
these measured tracks

this porous hollow
where light refracts
and insight begins

this ground-swell, this mole
this rich black vein
calls us, calls us home

—Scott Wiggerman

Craft Tip #29: Making More of Revision

—Diane Lockward

During revision discussions, we poets hear about compression, reducing clutter, and cutting out the non-essential. Who hasn't sat in a poetry class or workshop and been told that *less is more?* So when someone tells us to add more, to expand, to keep going, we might be hesitant to pay attention.

But we should pay attention. The less-is-more principle is often good advice, but it's not *always* good advice. As I once heard Mark Doty say, *Sometimes more is more.*

Too often we start revising and hacking away at the poem before it's even fully written. We quit before we've given the poem life, before we've discovered its full potential, before we've found its real material.

Stephen Dunn addresses the topic of revision in a 2007 interview in *The Pedestal Magazine:*

> A fairly new experience that I've been having is revision as expansion. Most of us know about revision as an act of paring down. Several years ago, in looking at my work, I saw that I was kind of a page or page and a half kind of poet, which meant that I was thinking of closure around the same time in every poem. I started to confound that habit. By mid-poem, I might add a detail that the poem couldn't yet accommodate. That's especially proven to be an interesting and useful way of revising poems that seem too slight or thin; to add something, put an obstacle in. The artificial as another way to arrive at the genuine—an old story, really.

Revision as expansion? Take Dunn's words to heart. Before you begin to strip down your poem or abandon it as no good or decide it's good enough as it is, first consider how you might expand your poem. The following expansion strategies just might help you to discover your poem's true potential and *arrive at the genuine.*

1. Choose a single poem by someone else, one that has strong diction. Take ten words from that poem and, in no particular order, plug them into your own draft. Make them make sense within the context of your poem, adjusting your context as needed. Or let the words introduce an element of the strange, a touch of the surreal.

2. Find the lifeless part of your poem. This is often the part where your mind begins to wander when you read the poem aloud. Open up space there and keep on writing in that space. Repeat elsewhere if needed. Remember that freewriting can occur not only while drafting but also while revising.

3. Find three places in the poem where you could insert a negative statement. Then go into the right margin of your draft and write those statements. Add them to the poem. By being contrary, you might add depth and richness to the poem.

4. Go into the right margin and write some kind of response to each line, perhaps its opposite, perhaps a question. The material that you add to the right margin might very well be your best material, the real material. Bring what works into the poem. Make friends with the right margin; good things happen out there.

5. Put something into your poem that seemingly doesn't belong, perhaps some kind of food, a tree, a piece of furniture, a policeman, or a dog. Elaborate.

6. Add a color and exploit it throughout the poem. This is often a surprisingly effective enlivening strategy, one that can alter the tone of the poem.

7. Go metaphor crazy. Add ten metaphors or similes to the poem. Keep the keepers.

8. Look up the vocabulary of an esoteric subject that has nothing to do with your poem. The subject might be mushroom foraging, astronomy, cryogenics, perfume-making, bee keeping, the Argentinian tango, or zombies. Make a list of at least ten words. Include a variety of parts of speech. Import the words into your poem. Develop as needed.

9. Pick any one concrete object in your poem and personify it throughout the poem. For example, if there's a rock, give it feelings, let it observe and think, give it a voice. As the object comes alive, so may the poem.

10. Midway or two-thirds into your poem, insert a story, perhaps something from the newspaper, a book you've read, a fable, or a fairy tale. Don't use the entire story, just enough of it to add some texture and weight to your poem. Your challenge is to find the connection between this new material and what was already in the poem.

Now go into your folder of old, abandoned poems, the ones you gave up on when you decided they just weren't going anywhere. Then get out some of your recent poems that feel merely good enough, the ones that never gave you that jolt of excitement we get when a poem is percolating. Finally, return to some of the poems that you've submitted and submitted with no success, those poor rejects.

Mark all of these poems as once again *in progress*. Now apply some of the expansion strategies and see if you can breathe new life into the poems. Remember that this kind of revision is not a matter of merely making the poem longer; it's a matter of making the poem better.

Poem and Prompt

Omniscient Love

He was in knocking range of my secrets.
He had found kelp there,
he nested in the coral beds.
In a past life he was born
to me as a set of twins.
He was applied to me as a topical ointment.
He was a prescient code,
a secret writing shaped into flesh.
He was the fathomer I never expected,
the pillow talk of the bureaucracy,
the breeze that could carry the world off-course.
It was as if we'd always believed in each other precisely,
and even the clouds agreed,
and the dog and his bone;
every particle of language
jumped like a flea around him. He was
a pirate's nautical exercise
and an argument for the resurrection.
He was in every seed bed
and digression.
He was bending down my angels and breasting
the seas of goldenmost wheat.
To ask for everything and get it
seemed a paltry thing
next to being recognized by him.
A button couldn't pop
but he was there with a net.

—Lee Upton

I admire the playfulness and the strangeness of this extravagant love poem. Loaded with metaphors and hyperboles, it epitomizes the language of love. Upton uses kaleidoscopic metaphors, i.e., wide-ranging and exhaustive ones. Her hyperboles strain the bounds of what is possible, e.g., *every particle of language / jumped like a flea around him*. How else to describe the perfection of this beyond perfection beloved!

Notice the structure of the poem. We get a series of declarative sentences, many beginning with the anaphoric *He was* followed by a metaphor. The similar sentence structure and the anaphora add rhythm and underscore both the accumulation of metaphors and the beloved's many virtues. Notice, too, that some of the sentences contain multiple metaphors. While the single metaphor, *He was applied to me as a topical ointment*, stands alone, the next two sentences each contain a series of metaphors: *He was a prescient code, / a secret writing shaped into flesh. / He was the fathomer I never expected, / the pillow talk of the bureaucracy, / the breeze that could carry the world off-course.*

Just when her pattern might have become predictable, Upton varies it. For example, line 4 begins with a prepositional phrase. Line 12 drops the *He* and begins with *It was as if we'd...* Line 23 begins with an infinitive. The last two lines again alter the pattern as that sentence begins with a noun rather than a pronoun, uses an active verb rather than a form of *to be*, and is a compound sentence.

For your new poem, first choose something or someone you feel passionate about, e.g., brussel sprouts, your baby, your rival, a tomato, your pet, the friend or lover who betrayed you or saved you, body fat.

Now write a draft in which you describe your subject in metaphors. Pile them on, one after the other. Be extravagant and hyperbolic. Try for at least a dozen figures. (You can later delete the losers and add some new winners.)

Remember to employ words that lead to hyperbole: *always, everything, every, most, least, never, all*, or any other superlatives.

Several drafts in, begin to pay attention to the structure of your poem. Set up a pattern of declarative sentences. Make your speaker sound firm and resolute. Use some anaphora. Once you have set up a pattern, be sure to break it here and there.

You might keep your poem to a single dense stanza or break it into several stanzas. Indentations might be fun to try.

Sample Poems

Intrinsic

If you were hands on a harpsichord, I'd read the mind
of Bach, the score of human heaven, while relishing all you
weren't playing, but could. If I were blind, I'd hear

the density, the textures you sculpt in air.
If you were me, I'd love you haphazardly,
subjectively, never believing that you sound,

look, act as you do. If I were deaf, your speed,
refraction of light from motions, would speak.
If you were a sheltering barn, I'd invest in your sanctuary,

comfort space you reserve under rain, sun, stars,
smells of shuffling warmth and cured harvest,
subtle advance up your sides of fungi lace,

weeds leaning, wildflowers opening, closing
against you: jewel set in meadow.
If I could not move, I'd dance before, dance after

the voice of your breath, encapsulating your touches;
my actions would sprout from your vision—
the love you wish to give, the love you perceive.

If you were ocean, I'd reverse evolution—
my arms and legs, to fins and tail,
you the water I breathe to live.

—Maren Mitchell

What Kind of Dog Is He? He's Brown

You are my triple word score,
my pharmacy within, my licking
tears before they fall, excuse to run,
hot water bottle, mahogany table in sunlight,
various grains, two hundred fifty golds and browns.
You're what all other dogs would resemble in fifty years
if we stopped breeding them. You, my cool cloth on forehead,
smell of woodsmoke, perfect grilled cheese. You, my lowered pressure.

So soft for so old.
I love how you love me best,
whimper if we part ways on a family walk.
I'm touched that when I travel, you mope around
looking for a rope to hang yourself, or so my husband says.

When mornings hurt, I love to lie
on the floor at your feet,
you who lick my late night sweats away.

—Tina Kelley

Craft Tip #30: Sometimes, Beware the Good Poem

—Dick Allen

Donald Hall doesn't recall saying it or writing it or, if he did, where he said or wrote it, but I remember. It went something like this: *Every major poem is likely to contain at least one serious flaw.*

True or not, if you keep this observation in mind, you may be able to stop yourself from committing one of the greatest sins of contemporary poetry writing, which is the sin of over-revision— that arch-sin arising out of listening overly hard to suggestions from a mentor or other participants in a poetry workshop.

It's rather Zen: *Listen and don't listen at once.*

Over-revision tends to tamp down a poem, to suck out its life, to leave in it too little of its original passion. No?

Imagine T. S. Eliot listening to his fellows in a poetry workshop and restarting his "Love Song of J. Alfred Prufrock," with proper grammar: *Let us go then, you and me...*

Imagine John Keats slapping the palm of his hand to his temple when a historian points out that in "On First Looking into Chapman's Homer" the lines should be, *Or like stout Balboa when with eagle eyes / He star'd at the Pacific...*

Once, when I was conducting an Independent Studies course with a young poet who has since published many poems in leading magazines, I was distressed by his use of *plover* in a new poem. *Plover*, I told him, was really an ugly name for a bird. So I showed him how to revise the poem, taking out *plover* and substituting *thrush* or *sparrow* or a bird of another feather. We worked over the poem, revising, changing, following its assonance and alliteration and line breaks and the like.

After about a half hour of this (I even typed up the consequent new version on my office Smith-Corona), we looked down at the poem, looked at each other, and simultaneously realized we'd totally ruined it. And my student never could get the poem back. *Mea culpa.*

At several stages in writing a poem, it's wise to ask yourself, *Is this too perfect?* and *Is there anything wrong about my poem?* and *Does it seem like an architect's blueprint, too polished, exact, correct—and bland? Where's the Evil?*

Co-judging a poetry contest with Joseph Parisi when he was editing *Poetry*, I was startled when Parisi emitted a downright *No!* to a poem the other co-judge and I both thought excellent. Parisi flatly commented that *Poetry* received scores of similar poems every week. The poem we thought excellent, Parisi said, was—alas—*excellent.*

That was what was wrong with it. The poet had neglected Emerson's admonition: *Your goodness must have some edge to it—lest it is none.*

The poem was overcooked. It was dull. It was boring. No touch of strange. No wildebeest to roam its corners. No Zen to upset us. No flaw that might make the form which contained it—just as legendary Persian carpets purposely contain an errant thread—storm us away. It was—*excellent.*

Here's another way to remember this advice. Emerson again: *In every work of genius we recognize our own rejected thoughts; they come back to us with a certain alienated majesty.*

Hundreds of times I've gone over beginning drafts of poems in workshops and in manuscripts sent to me, and been enthralled by what the poems are doing, how they're sounding, what they're reaching toward, what craft they're demonstrating.

And hundreds of times, as the poem gets revised, I've seen it deflate. It gets better and better technically, but something fades. An essential rawness or quirk or even an accidental stumble gets written out. The resultant cleaned-up poem smiles too much as it happily or sadly shows itself off.

Beware your own skills. Beware in your own writing and in working with poems of others the understandable impulse to cast out the flaw too quickly.

As you work your poem through, keep all the drafts. If by the second or third draft something feels wrong, go back to the first draft and find what it was that might have made your hair stand on end. If you've revised that thing out, try putting it back in no matter how awkward or wrong it feels. Alternately, toss the second and third drafts and start the poem again with the first lines of the first draft.

Or if you've finished the poem, if you've received mild applause for it from a workshop, if you've more or less satisfied everyone and been rewarded by murmurs of approval, you may have to toss it.

Yeats wrote, in "The Fisherman," of *A man who does not exist, / A man who is but a dream*. But in the poem's closure, the narrator cries,

> Before I am old
> I shall have written him one
> Poem maybe as cold
> And passionate as the dawn.

To ask of ourselves anything less than to keep such an ideal before us is to let our mediocre efforts stand unchallenged. If at least in the back of our minds we're able to let go of the *fine*, or the *good enough*, or the *it works*, or the *excellent*, we might someday write the one poem that riddles us with wonder and puts all of our other poems to shame.

Poem and Prompt

Relax

Bad things are going to happen.
Your tomatoes will grow a fungus
and your cat will get run over.
Someone will leave the bag with the ice cream
melting in the car and throw
your blue cashmere sweater in the drier.
Your husband will sleep
with a girl your daughter's age, her breasts spilling
out of her blouse. Or your wife
will remember she's a lesbian
and leave you for the woman next door. The other cat—
the one you never really liked—will contract a disease
that requires you to pry open its feverish mouth
every four hours. Your parents will die.
No matter how many vitamins you take,
how much Pilates, you'll lose your keys,
your hair, and your memory. If your daughter
doesn't plug her heart
into every live socket she passes,
you'll come home to find your son has emptied
the refrigerator, dragged it to the curb,
and called the used-appliance store for a pick up—drug money.
The Buddha tells a story of a woman chased by a tiger.
When she comes to a cliff, she sees a sturdy vine
and climbs halfway down. But there's also a tiger below.
And two mice—one white, one black—scurry out
and begin to gnaw at the vine. At this point
she notices a wild strawberry growing from a crevice.
She looks up, down, at the mice.
Then she eats the strawberry.
So here's the view, the breeze, the pulse
in your throat. Your wallet will be stolen, you'll get fat,

slip on the bathroom tiles in a foreign hotel
and crack your hip. You'll be lonely.
Oh, taste how sweet and tart
the red juice is, how the tiny seeds
crunch between your teeth.

—Ellen Bass

The speaker in Bass's poem begins with a stark declarative statement, sort of like a thesis statement. She then sets about proving or illustrating the truth of that opening statement. We get a laundry list of bad things, some of them trivial, some of them very significant.

The poem is addressed to *you*, but a general you; it could be me, it could be you. It could be female (the *you* has a husband who *will sleep / with a girl your daughter's age*); it could be male (the *you* has a wife who *will remember she's a lesbian / and leave you for the woman next door*). Nevertheless, that *you* makes us feel spoken to.

This poem intrigues me with its use of the future tense. The bad things haven't yet happened, but they *will* happen. Think about how the poem would change if the poet had used present tense: *Bad things happen. / Your tomatoes grow a fungus / and your cat gets run over.* Or if she had used past tense: *Bad things happened. / Your tomatoes grew a fungus / and your cat was run over.* What happens to the tone when the verb tense is changed?

I'm also intrigued by the Buddhist story that gets inserted into the poem towards the end and by the shift there to present tense. This story transforms the poem and leads to what seems almost like a moral, except that it's expressed in a stunning image: *Oh, taste how sweet and tart / the red juice is, how the tiny seeds / crunch between your teeth.* The image is so much more effective than if the poet had said something explicit like *Live fully in the moment, no matter where you are, no matter the circumstances.*

Now go back to the title. So simple. Just one word. After we've read the poem, the title takes on weight. *Relax* is perhaps all we can do in the certainty that bad things are going to happen.

For your own poem, begin by making a list of bad things that could possibly happen. Be serious. Be playful. Your list can be broad as it is in Bass's poem or it can be narrow, e.g., lost things, mistakes made, accidents, injuries, things that decayed.

Begin your draft with a declarative statement. Then include the items from your list. After twenty or so lines, insert a brief story. This might be something from mythology, the Bible, history, family history, or something a teacher or a friend once told you. It might take you several days to come up with an appropriate story. Be patient; it will come.

After you've inserted your story, swing back to your list and pull in a few more items. End with an image that emerges from the story.

As you revise your draft, consider verb tense. If you have future, fiddle with past and present and see what happens.

Consider also your direct address. What would happen if, instead of addressing the anonymous *you*, you had someone specific in mind, perhaps even addressed that person by name? What would happen if the *you* became *I*, or *he, she, we*, or *they*?

Sample Poems

Don't Fight It

Just face it. You're going to die.
You're going to fall down the stairs
and split your head. You're going to be
a passenger on the jetliner that vanishes.
You're going to stumble and fall in front
of a tractor-trailer. At the hospital
you will be infected with flesh-eating bacteria.
Or you will eat contaminated
spinach. Or that sweet little shih-tzu next door
will get bitten by a rabid raccoon
and attack you.
The fact that you eat all organic, plenty
of fruits and vegetables, work out three times
a week will do nothing to prevent your horse
from crashing through a jump and crushing you,
or that black widow spider from crawling
into your sleeping bag.
Your husband will give you HIV
from a rendezvous with a Las Vegas "lady,"
or your wife will forget to tell you
that the third floor balcony railing is loose.
My mother told a story about her uncle's
first Model T, and how it slid
off a muddy road one day, down a bank
into a stream, and all her uncle
worried about was getting at least one sip
from his broken case of champagne.
So here's the program: you will be asphyxiated
by a carbon monoxide leak. You will drown
when you slip and fall in the tub. A piece

of space junk will fall, flaming from the sky.
You will have a heart attack out running
when a truck full of Miller Light explodes
all over you, but oh, that final taste
of perfection.

—Patricia L. Goodman
published in *The Broadkill Review*

Kabob

Bad, no-good, terrible things
are going to happen.
Your gums will recede,
your underpants lose
their elastic, your dog
grow old and incontinent.
You'll bury the generation
ahead of you, become next in line,
no one to buffer you from the abyss.
No matter how many Warriors you do,
or horse-sized calcium pills
you swallow, your skin will
speckle and droop, your hair
turn the color of February.
You'll misplace everything,
drugstore glasses on your head,
word on the tip of your tongue,
the reason you came into a room,
or why you were ever angry
with your brother
in the first place. Your daughter will
get tattooed, your son leave home
without even an ungrateful note.
Rumi writes about being a burnt kabob.
Thirst drove him to the water where he
drank the moon's reflection,
his body a ruin, like overcooked
meat on a skewer. His heart
was a donkey sunk in a mudhole.
Like you, widowed to loss,
you, with this string of diminuendo,
teeth and strength and breath itself.
But hear the admonishment:
the silent music of blossoms
as they depart the tree, scattering
petals everywhere.

—Barbara G. S. Hagerty

The Poet on the Poem: Lance Larsen

To Jouissance

To spell you is to drown in vowels, to pronounce
you is to let guttural *joy* form in the back
of my throat, then roll forth,
like northern lights booming above a logging
camp in Michigan. Disappointed
in my metaphor? What did you expect from a man?

If only I had an estrogen factory of my own.
If only I could feel the fluttery,
everywhere *she*-pleasure you bring to lucky
women. I mean the buzz that overtakes
a new mother nursing in a booth at Denny's,
eyes blissing out, body serenely electric.

I mean whatever state my cousin Erica falls
into when someone braids her hair
in the middle of church—simple Erica
who washes tables at McDonald's
but can't read a menu. She knows
enough to close her eyes and give pleasure

more room, knows enough to let purrs
bubble from her mouth, the liquid gold
on her head dividing into glorious threes,
my jealousy tripling. Do you sometimes
make exceptions and visit not just
the Ericas of the world, but the Erics?

I'm thinking of the twenty-something kid
last week who popped up from his seat
and ran to the front of the bus.
That's my old man, he said, pointing
to the cement truck stopped beside us
at a red light. *Hey Dad, I'm over here, look,*

and Ernie, our glum undertaker of a driver,
broke the rules for once and swung
open the door at the intersection.
Surely you must have blessed that transaction:
grizzled duffer and tattooed boy leaning
towards each other, like a pair of gargoyles,

air crackling between them. The light turned
green, the afternoon sped up, and the duffer
said, *Hey Tommy, nice hat, you ready*
for bowling Saturday night?—take her easy.
Who can explain where the world ends and a son
begins, how molecules of desire map the body?

They waved, father and son, like they'd never
see each other again in this time zone.
And we watched: hungry, eavesdropping citizens
of the bus, remembering some ecstasy
we fell into once and didn't deserve, sitting
on our hands to keep from adding amens to the air.

DL: I admire this poem for the risks it takes. I'm struck, for example, by the audacity of titling the poem with a word that most likely almost nobody knows. Why an ode to *jouissance*?

LL: Ever since discovering the term in a French feminism class at Rice University, I've been fascinated by *jouissance*—the notion that women enjoy a less localized, more all-pervasive evolution of pleasure. How could I not be fascinated? It's a pretty heady experience to read Cixous, Kristeva, and Luce Irigaray for the first time. My title might be off-putting to some, at least at first, but I'm old-fashioned enough to believe that readers, especially of poetry, have dictionaries attached to their bodies the way they have eyelashes and ears.

The challenge was to write a poem that dramatizes the differences between male and female desire in such a way that the reader doesn't need a dictionary at all. Whether I've pulled that off is a separate question. I'm not entirely clear now what got me to the title. Either I started with *jouissance* and canvassed my brain for the kind of sensory detail that would bring the term alive. Or I had these unshakeable sensory impressions and went looking for the appropriate catalyst that would allow Erica and Eric to co-exist in the same poem. While the conceptual dimension of a poem is crucial, the particulars are what provide ballast and launch: the sound of the words, the image, the metaphors, the syntax, the sublime grit that sticks a poem to the page.

DL: Tell us about your use of direct address and the function of the questions you pose to Jouissance.

LL: One can write moving odes in third person, but these often tend towards a chaste distance poetically—observation rather than drama. I like the intimacy one gains with direct address. Apostrophe is one of the most shamelessly artificial of literary devices but it pulls us in nonetheless, and the great poets are not above using it. Think, for instance, of Keats in "Ode on a Grecian Urn": *What men or gods are these? What maidens loth? / What mad pursuit? What struggle to escape?* Most odes have a circular quality to them, an argument that moves away from the speaker and then returns. Direct address helps to facilitate this movement of thinking on the page.

DL: Your speaker straddles the line between rudeness and kindness as he names his cousin *simple Erica* but then transforms her into the dispenser of pleasure, someone who *purrs* and has *liquid gold / on her head*. Tell us about the craft that went into this balance.

LL: As a beginning writer, I was driven by a search for felicitous language and image. While I've never abandoned these pursuits, I'm increasingly interested in shifts in tone and contradiction, in irony. I like flawed speakers who get themselves into a little trouble, as this narrator does. By condescending to Erica—he digs a hole for himself, which he then has to crawl out of. Of course, in his double mindedness, he introduces an Erica that is more contradictory and multivalent, more human, than if he had settled for a character of simple sweetness and light. In a way, the poem dramatizes the dangers of overthinking—that is, of privileging book smarts over more authentic primary experience.

In the end, the narrator ends up envying Erica for her life of sensation, for her ability to give herself to simple pleasures, pleasures which I hope the reader can taste in the language of the poem.

DL: At the midway point you skillfully turn the poem, moving from the feminine to the masculine. In effect, your speaker gets what he wants and makes Jouissance do his bidding. How did you contrive to make the poem turn so smoothly?

LL: Perhaps that turn is more my lucking into something. In the middle of a draft, frustrated because I didn't know what should come next, I noticed that the word *Eric* (which happens to be my middle name) was embedded in *Erica*. An obvious thing to most readers but it wasn't to me. I love the story about Yeats reading final galleys of one of his books. In describing a woman's face, he had written *mass of shadows*, but his phrase came back from the printer as *mess of shadows*. He was wise enough to keep the mistake. Poems often know more than their creators, and when we're wise enough, we know when to keep mistakes and serendipitous accidents. The poem may turn smoothly, but this doesn't mean we should trust it—at least not completely. Some readers may see this final move in the poem as a kind of male appropriation, which doesn't bother me in the least. The poem is about vicarious experience. About being in one body and many bodies simultaneously. Or wanting to be. Though the poem ends in celebration, I'm well aware that it begins in lack. In other words, I'm open to an ironic and more skeptical reading.

DL: There's a formal elegance to this poem. You have eight 6-line stanzas and fairly even line lengths. At what point in writing the poem did you decide to use 6-line stanzas? What manipulations had to occur?

LL: I committed to 6-line stanzas midway in the writing after I had much but not all of the poem's language. This decision propelled the poem through an additional series of revisions. I tightened and re-configured, cutting whenever possible. I'm one who winnows and distills down. Regular stanzas invited me to see the poem as a series of crescendoes and pauses accumulating over two pages: how to make that progression as organic as possible? I always work for a mix of end-stopped and enjambed lines, which replicates breathing and movement, hesitation and lunge.

I like this stage of revision, not unlike my father tying flies, which he used to do late in the evening. Without the close work of tweezers and magnifying glass, I know I've got little more than chopped prose. If one of my lines fails to surprise me, if a stanza isn't compelling in its own right regardless of the larger task it's doing in the poem, then I have more work to do.

Bonus Prompt: The Echoing Vowel Poem

Choose a vowel, long or short, and make a list of ten words with that vowel sound. For example, if you choose long *i* as your vowel, you might begin your list with *live* and then develop a list something like the following:

live
wild
blind
slide
file
pride
mind
shy
applied
wife

Avoid straight rhymes. Keeping that guideline in mind, the above list could not include *hive* or *five*.

Once you have your list, write a 20-line poem with one of the words used in every other line. The words should be scattered rather than used at the end of each line.

Contributors

Kelli Russell Agodon is the author of four poetry books, most recently *Hourglass Museum* (White Pine, 2014). She has won awards from Artist Trust, The Puffin Foundation, and *North American Review*. She is co-founder and editor of Two Sylvias Press.

Dick Allen served as the Connecticut State Poet Laureate from 2010-2015. He is the author of eight collections of poetry, most recently *This Shadowy Place*, winner of the 2013 *New Criterion* Poetry Prize. His work has earned inclusion in six volumes of *The Best American Poetry* and fellowships from the NEA and the Ingram Merrill Foundation.

Nin Andrews is the author of six chapbooks and six full-length poetry collections, including *Why God Is a Woman* (BOA, 2015). She has won two Ohio individual artist grants, the Pearl Chapbook Contest, the Kent State University chapbook contest, and the Gerald Cable Poetry Award.

David Barber is the author of two collections of poems, most recently *Wonder Cabinet* (Northwestern UP, 2006). He is poetry editor of *The Atlantic* and has received grants and fellowships from the NEA, the Massachusetts Cultural Council, and PEN New England. He teaches in the Harvard Writing Program.

Judith Barrington is the author of four poetry collections, most recently *The Conversation* (Salmon). Her *Lifesaving: A Memoir* won the Lambda Book Award and was a finalist for the PEN/Martha Albrand Award. She served on the faculty of the University of Alaska's MFA program.

Ellen Bass is the author of three poetry books, most recently *Like a Beggar* (Copper Canyon, 2014). Her awards include fellowships from the NEA and the California Arts Council and two Pushcart Prizes. She teaches in the low-residency MFA program at Pacific University.

Mary Biddinger is the author of four collections of poetry, most recently *A Sunny Place with Adequate Water* (Black Lawrence, 2014). Editor of *Barn Owl Review*, the Akron Series in Poetry, and the Akron Series in Contemporary Poetics, she also teaches poetry writing and literature at the University of Akron.

George Bilgere has published six poetry collections, most recently *Imperial*. He has received awards and fellowships from the Pushcart Foundation, the NEA, the Fulbright Foundation, and the Witter Bynner Foundation. His poems have been featured in *The Writer's Almanac* and *American Life in Poetry*.

Chana Bloch is the author of books of poetry, translation, and scholarship. Her latest book is *Swimming in the Rain: New and Selected Poems, 1980-2015*. She is the recipient of two fellowships from the NEA, a fellowship from the National Endowment for the Humanities, and the Discovery Award of the 92nd Street Y Poetry Center. She is Professor Emerita of English at Mills College.

Laure-Anne Bosselaar is the author of *The Hour Between Dog and Wolf, Small Gods of Grief*, which won the Isabella Gardner Prize for Poetry, and *A New Hunger*. The editor of four anthologies and the recipient of a Pushcart Prize, she is a core faculty member in the Solstice Low-Residency MFA in Creative Writing Program.

David Bottoms served as Poet Laureate of Georgia for twelve years. He is the author of eight books of poetry, most recently *We Almost Disappear*. Among his awards are an Ingram Merrill Award and fellowships from the NEA and the Guggenheim Foundation. He holds the Amos Distinguished Chair in English Letters at Georgia State University.

Fleda Brown served as Poet Laureate of Delaware from 2001-2007. She is the author of eight poetry collections, most recently *No Need of Sympathy*. Her awards include the Felix Pollak Prize, the Philip Levine Prize, and the Great Lakes Colleges New Writers Award. She teaches in the Rainier Writing Workshop at Pacific Lutheran University.

Kathryn Stripling Byer served from 2005-2009 as North Carolina's first woman Poet Laureate. She is the author of six poetry collections, most recently *Descent*. Her awards include the Hanes Poetry Award from the Fellowship of Southern Writers, the Southern Independent Booksellers Alliance Poetry Award, and the Roanoke-Chowan Award.

Lauren Camp is the author of three books, most recently *One Hundred Hungers*, winner of the Dorset Prize (Tupelo Press, 2016). Her honors include the Margaret Randall Poetry Prize, an Anna Davidson Rosenberg Award, and a Black Earth Institute Fellowship. She produces and hosts "Audio Saucepan" on Santa Fe Public Radio.

Martha Collins is the author of eight books of poetry, most recently *Admit One: An American Scrapbook* (U of Pittsburgh, 2016). Her awards include fellowships from the NEA, the Bunting Institute, the Ingram Merrill Foundation, and the Witter Bynner Foundation, as well as three Pushcart Prizes.

Mary Cornish, a former children's book illustrator, is the author of the poetry collection *Red Studio,* which won the 2006 Field Poetry Prize from Oberlin College Press. She is a former Wallace Stegner Fellow and teaches creative writing at Western Washington University.

Oliver de la Paz is the author of four collections of poetry, most recently *Post Subject: A Fable* (U of Akron, 2014). A recipient of a New York Foundation Fellowship and a GAP grant from Artists' Trust, he teaches at Holy Cross and in the low-residency MFA program at PLU.

Carl Dennis has published twelve books of poetry, including *Another Reason* (Penguin, 2014). His *Practical Gods* (Penguin, 2001) won the Pulitzer Prize. His awards include fellowships from the Guggenheim Foundation and the NEA and the Ruth Lilly Poetry Prize. He taught at the University of Buffalo and now serves as the school's artist-in-residence.

Toi Derricotte is the author of *The Undertaker's Daughter* (U of Pittsburgh, 2011) and four earlier collections of poetry. Her honors include the 2012 PEN/Voelcker Award, two Pushcart Prizes, and the Distinguished Pioneering of the Arts Award. She is the co-founder of the Cave Canem Foundation, Professor Emerita at the University of Pittsburgh, and a Chancellor of the Academy of American Poets.

Natalie Diaz is the author of *When My Brother Was an Aztec* (Copper Canyon, 2012). Her awards include the Nimrod/Hardman Pablo Neruda Prize for Poetry, the Narrative Poetry Prize, and a Lannan Literary Fellowship. Her publications include *Best New Poets, Prairie Schooner*, and *Crab Orchard Review*.

Camille Dungy is the author of three collections, most recently *Smith Blue* (Southern Illinois UP, 2011), which won the 2010 Crab Orchard Open Book Prize. Her honors include an American Book Award, a Sustainable Arts Foundation grant, and a fellowship from the NEA. She is an English Professor at Colorado State University.

Jill Alexander Essbaum is the author of several collections of poetry, including *Heaven*, which won the Bakeless Poetry Prize. She is the recipient of two NEA literature fellowships and is a member of the core faculty at the University of California, Riverside.

Alice B. Fogel is the Poet Laureate of New Hampshire (2014-2019). She is the author of three poetry collections, most recently *Interval: Poems Based on Bach's Goldberg Variations*, which won the Nicholas Schaffner Award. Her honors include an NEA fellowship and the New England Poetry Club's Daniel Varoujan Award. She teaches at Keene State College.

Alice Friman's sixth collection is *The View from Saturn* (LSU, 2014). For her previous collection, *Vinculum*, she won the 2012 Georgia Author of the Year Award in Poetry. She is a recipient of a 2012 Pushcart Prize, is included in *The Best American Poetry*, and is Poet-in-Residence at Georgia College.

Karin Gottshall is the author of *The River Won't Hold You*, which won the Ohio State University Press/The Journal Wheeler Prize. Her first book, *Crocus*, won the Poets Out Loud Prize in 2007 and was published by Fordham University Press. She teaches at Middlebury College.

Tami Haaland served as Montana's Poet Laureate from 2013-2015. She is the author of two books of poetry, most recently *When We Wake in the Night*. She has received an Innovation Award from the Montana Arts Council and grants from Humanities Montana. She is a professor of English at Montana State University Billings.

Barbara Hamby is the author of five poetry collections, most recently *On the Street of Divine Love: New and Selected Poems* (U of Pittsburgh, 2014). She has won fellowships from the Guggenheim Foundation and the NEA. In 2010, she was named a Distinguished University Scholar at Florida State University.

Ava Leavell Haymon is the former Poet Laureate of Louisiana. Her most recent poetry collection is *Eldest Daughter* (LSU, 2013). Her prizes include the Louisiana Literature Prize for poetry, the L. E. Phillabaum Poetry Award, and the Mississippi Institute of Arts and Letters Award in Poetry.

Tom Hennen is the author of *Darkness Sticks to Everything: Collected and New Poems* (Copper Canyon, 2013). He is the recipient of the Bachelor Farmer Lifetime Achievement Award in the Arts. He helped found the Minnesota Writers Publishing House.

David Hernandez is the author of four poetry collections, including *Dear, Sincerely* (Pitt Poetry Series, 2016) and *Hoodwinked* (Sarabande, 2011), which won the Kathryn A. Morton Prize in Poetry. His awards include an NEA fellowship and a Pushcart Prize. He teaches creative writing at California State University.

Tony Hoagland is the author of five volumes of poetry, most recently *Application for Release from the Dream* (Graywolf, 2015). He is the recipient of fellowships from the NEA, the Poetry Foundation's Mark Twain Award, and the Jackson Poetry Prize. He teaches at the University of Houston.

Karla Huston is the author of *A Theory of Lipstick* (Main Street Rag, 2013) and seven chapbooks. She is the recipient of a Pushcart Prize and has appeared in *The Pushcart Prize: Best of the Small Presses* (2012). She teaches poetry writing workshops at The Mill: A Place for Writers in Wisconsin.

Laura Kasischke has published eight books of poetry, most recently *The Infinitesimals*. She has received Guggenheim and NEA fellowships, several Pushcart Prizes, and the 2012 National Book Critics Circle Award for

Poetry. She is the Allan Seager Professor of English Language & Literature at the University of Michigan.

Meg Kearney is the author of two poetry books, most recently *Home by Now* (Four Way Books, 2009), winner of the 2010 PEN New England L.L. Winship Award. She is Founding Director of the Solstice Low-Residency MFA in Creative Writing Program at Pine Manor College.

David Kirby is the author of more than two dozen volumes of criticism, essays, children's literature, pedagogy, and poetry. His awards include fellowships from the Guggenheim Foundation and the NEA, and several Pushcart Prizes. He teaches at Florida State University.

Lance Larsen was appointed Poet Laureate of Utah in 2012. He is the author of four collections of poems, most recently *Genius Loci* (U of Tampa, 2013). His work has been published in *The Georgia Review, The Southern Review, The Pushcart Prize Anthology,* and elsewhere. He teaches literature and creative writing at BYU and serves as associate chair.

Sydney Lea is the former Poet Laureate of Vermont. He has published twelve volumes of poetry, including *No Doubt the Nameless* (Four Way Books, 2016). He has also published a novel and four volumes of nonfiction. He is the recipient of fellowships from the MacArthur, Rockefeller, and Fulbright Foundations.

Ada Limón is the author of four collections of poetry, most recently *Bright Dead Things* (Milkweed, 2015). She has received fellowships from the Provincetown Fine Arts Work Center and the New York Foundation for the Arts. Her work has appeared in such publications as *Harvard Review, TriQuarterly Online,* and *The New Yorker.*

Timothy Liu is the author of several collections of poetry, most recently *Don't Go Back to Sleep* (Saturnalia, 2014). HIs awards include the Poetry Society of America's Norma Farber First Book Award, a Pushcart Prize, and the Open Book Beyond Margins Award. He is an associate professor at William Paterson University.

Alessandra Lynch is the author of two collections of poetry, most recently *It was a terrible cloud at twilight,* winner the Lena-Miles Wever Todd Award from Pleiades Press. A recipient of a Barbara Deming Memorial Award, she has received fellowships from Yaddo and MacDowell. She teaches at Butler University.

Davis McCombs is the author of three poetry collections, most recently *lore,* which received the 2015 Agha Shahid Ali Prize in Poetry (U of Utah P, 2016). He is the recipient of fellowships from the Ruth Lilly Poetry Foundation, the Kentucky Arts Council, and the NEA. He teaches in the Creative Writing Program at the University of Arkansas.

Susan Laughter Meyers is the author of two poetry books, most recently *My Dear, Dear Stagger Grass* (2013), winner of the Cider Press Review Editors' Prize. Her work has been featured on *Poetry Daily, Verse Daily*, and Ted Kooser's *American Life in Poetry*.

Deborah A. Miranda is the author of *Bad Indians: A Tribal Memoir*, winner of the PEN Oakland Josephine Miles Literary Award and The Independent Publisher's Gold Medal. The author of three poetry collections and co-editor of *Sovereign Erotics: An Anthology of Two Spirit Literature*, she teaches at Washington and Lee University.

D. Nurkse is the author of ten collections of poetry, most recently *A Night in Brooklyn* (Alfred Knopf, 2016). He is the recipient of NEA and Guggenheim fellowships, the Whiting Writers Award, and prizes from the Poetry Foundation and the Tanne Foundation. He teaches at Sarah Lawrence College.

Priscilla Orr is the author of *Jugglers & Tides* and *Losing the Horizon*, both from Hannacroix Creek Books. She is the recipient of fellowships from the New Jersey State Council on the Arts and Yaddo. She is the founding Director of the Betty June Silconas Poetry Center and the founding editor of *The Stillwater Review*.

Paisley Rekdal is the author of five books of poetry, most recently *Imaginary Vessels* (Copper Canyon, 2016). Her awards include the Amy Lowell Poetry Traveling Fellowship, an NEA Fellowship, a Guggenheim Fellowship, a Fulbright Fellowship, and two Pushcart Prizes. She teaches at the University of Utah.

Susan Rich is the author of four collections of poetry, most recently *Cloud Pharmacy* (White Pine, 2014). Her awards include an Artist Trust Fellowship from Washington State and a Fulbright Fellowship in South Africa. Her poems have appeared in the *Antioch Review, Harvard Review*, and *TriQuarterly*.

Alberto Ríos served as the inaugural Poet Laureate of Arizona, 2013-2015. He is the author of thirteen books, most recently *A Small Story about the Sky* (Copper Canyon, 2015). He has received fellowships from the Guggenheim Foundation and the NEA, six Pushcart Prizes, and the Walt Whitman Award. He teaches at Arizona State University.

Lee Ann Roripaugh is the Poet Laureate of South Dakota, 2015-2019. She is the author of four volumes of poetry, most recently *Dandarians* (Milkweed, 2014). She won the 2004 Association of Asian American Studies Book Award in Poetry/Prose. She is a Professor of English at the University of South Dakota, Director of Creative Writing, and Editor-in-Chief of the *South Dakota Review*.

Sheryl St. Germain is the author of *Let it Be a Dark Roux: New and Selected Poems* (U of Utah, 2003). Her work has received two NEA Fellowships, an NEH Fellowship, and the William Faulkner Award for the personal essay. She directs the MFA program in Creative Writing at Chatham University in Pittsburgh.

Martha Silano is the author of four collections of poetry, most recently *Reckless Lovely* (Saturnalia, 2014). Her book, *The Little Office of the Immaculate Conception,* won the 2010 Saturnalia Poetry Prize. A recipient of fellowships from Seattle 4Culture and the Washington State Artist Trust, she teaches at Bellevue College.

Ron Smith is the former Poet Laureate of Virginia. He is the author of three collections, most recently *Its Ghostly Workshop* (LSU, 2013). In 2005 he was an inaugural winner of the Carole Weinstein Poetry Prize. He is Writer-in-Residence at St. Christopher's School in Richmond.

A. E. Stringer is the author of three collections of poems, most recently *Late Breaking* (Salmon, 2013). His work has appeared in such journals as *Prairie Schooner, Shenandoah,* and *Poetry Northwest.* He teaches writing and literature at Marshall University.

KC Trommer is the author of the chapbook *The Hasp Tongue* (dancing girl, 2014). The recipient of an Academy of American Poets Prize, she has been awarded fellowships from the Center for Book Arts, the Vermont Studio Center, the Haystack Mountain School of Crafts, and the Prague Summer Program.

William Trowbridge is the former Poet Laureate of Missouri. His latest collection, *Put This On, Please: New and Selected Poems,* was published by Red Hen Press. He teaches in the University of Nebraska low-residency MFA in writing program.

Lee Upton is the author of fourteen books of poetry and prose. Her sixth collection of poetry, *Bottle the Bottles the Bottles the Bottles,* was the recipient of the 2014 Open Book Award from the Cleveland State University Poetry Center. She is the Francis A. March Professor of English and Writer-in-Residence at Lafayette College.

Sidney Wade has published six books of poetry, most recently *Straits and Narrows: Poems* (Persea, 2013). A professor of English at the University of Florida, she edits the journal *Subtropics* and is a former president of the Association of Writers and Writing Programs.

Charles Harper Webb has published eight books of poetry, most recently *Brain Camp* (U of Pittsburgh, 2015). His awards include a Guggenheim fellowship, the Kate Tufts Discovery Award, and the Felix

Pollock Prize. A former professional rock musician and psychotherapist, he teaches creative writing at California State University, Long Beach.

Hilde Weisert is the author of *The Scheme of Things* (David Robert Books, 2015). Her poems have appeared in such journals as *Prairie Schooner*, *The Cincinnati Review*, and *Southern Poetry Review*. She is co-founder of the Society for Veterinary Medicine and Literature.

Marjory Wentworth is the Poet Laureate of South Carolina. She is the author of three books of poetry, most recently *The Endless Repetition of an Ordinary Miracle*. She is the current President of the Lowcountry Initiative for the Literary Arts (LILA) and teaches at The Art Institute of Charleston.

Terence Winch is the author of seven books of poetry, most recently *This Way Out* (Hanging Loose, 2014). He is also the author of two short story collections. He has received an NEA Fellowship in poetry, as well as grants from the District of Columbia Commission on the Arts and Humanities, the Maryland State Arts Council, and the Fund for Poetry.

Robert Wrigley is the author of nine collections of poetry, most recently *Anatomy of Melancholy* (Penguin, 2013). His awards include the Kingsley Tufts Award, the Poets' Prize, and the San Francisco Poetry Center Book Award. He has been the recipient of fellowships from the NEA and the Guggenheim Foundation.

Dean Young is the former Poet Laureate of Texas. He is the author of numerous collections of poetry, most recently *Shock by Shock* (Copper Canyon, 2015). His awards include fellowships from the Guggenheim Foundation, the NEA, and the Fine Arts Work Center. He teaches at the University of Texas-Austin.

Michael T. Young has published four collections of poetry, most recently *The Beautiful Moment of Being Lost* (Poets Wear Prada, 2014). His awards include a fellowship from the New Jersey State Council on the Arts and the Chaffin Poetry Award. His work has appeared in several journals, including *The Louisville Review, Off the Coast,* and *The Raintown Review.*

Credits

Index of Poets and Poems

About the Editor

Diane Lockward is the editor of *The Crafty Poet: A Portable Workshop* and the author of four poetry books, most recently *The Uneaten Carrots of Atonement* (Wind Publications, 2016). She is the recipient of the Quentin R. Howard Poetry Prize, a poetry fellowship from the New Jersey State Council on the Arts, and a Woman of Achievement Award. Her poems have been published in a number of anthologies, including *Poetry Daily: 366 Poems from the World's Most Popular Poetry Website* and Garrison Keillor's *Good Poems for Hard Times*. Her poems have also appeared in such journals as *Harvard Review*, *Southern Poetry Review*, and *Prairie Schooner*, and have been featured on *Poetry Daily*, *Verse Daily*, and *The Writer's Almanac*. She is the founder, editor, and publisher of Terrapin Books.